PRACTICAL SUGGESTIONS
for
MOTHER AND HOUSEWIFE

The 1910 classic—
as helpful now as it was then!

by
MARION MILLS MILLER

Edited by
THEODORE WATERS

RUNNING PRESS
PHILADELPHIA · LONDON

9   8   7   6   5   4   3   2   1
Digit on the right indicates the number of this printing

Library of Congress Control Number: 2008937080

ISBN 978-0-7624-3610-1

Cover and interior design by Frances J. Soo Ping Chow
Typography: Perpetua

Running Press Book Publishers
2300 Chestnut Street
Philadelphia, PA 19103-4371

Visit us on the web!
www.runningpress.com

PRACTICAL SUGGESTIONS

for

MOTHER AND HOUSEWIFE

Contents

husband and wife. Manipulating a husband. By deceit. By tact. Confidence between man and wife.

CHAPTER IV

THE HOUSE

Element in choice of a home. The city apartment. Furniture for a temporary home. Couches. Rugs. Book-cases. The suburban and country house. Economic considerations. Buying an old house. Building a new one. Supervising the building. The woman's wishes.

CHAPTER V

THE HOUSE

Essential parts of a house. Double use of rooms. Utility of piazzas. Landscape gardening. Water supply. Illumination. Dangers from gas. How to read a gas-meter. How to test kerosene. Care of lamps. Use of candles. Making the best of the old house.

CHAPTER VI

FURNITURE AND DECORATION

The qualities to be sought in furniture. Homemade furniture. Semi-made furniture. Good furniture as an investment. Furnishing and decorating the hall. The staircase. The parlor. Rugs and carpets. Oriental rugs. Floors. Treatment of hardwood. Of other wood. How to stain a floor covering.

CHAPTER VII

FURNITURE AND DECORATION

CHAPTER VIII

THE MOTHER

CHAPTER IX

THE MOTHER

CHAPTER X

CARE OF THE PERSON

CHAPTER XI

GENERAL PRINCIPLES OF COOKING

CHAPTER XII

GENERAL PRINCIPLES OF COOKING

CHAPTER XIII

RECIPES FOR MEAT DISHES

CHAPTER XIV

RECIPES FOR MEAT DISHES

CHAPTER XV

HOUSEHOLD RECIPES

Introduction

WHAT a tribute to the worth of a woman are the names by which she is enshrined in common speech! What tender associations halo the names of *wife, mother, sister,* and *daughter!* It must never be forgotten that the dearest, most sacred of these names, are, in origin, connected with the dignity of service. In early speech the wife, or wife-man (woman) was the "weaver," whose care it was to clothe the family, as it was the husband's duty to "feed" it, or to provide the materials of sustenance. The mother or matron was named from the most tender and sacred of human functions, the nursing of the babe; the daughter from her original duty, in the pastoral age, of milking of the cows. The lady was so-called from the social obligations entailed on the prosperous woman, of "loaf-giving," or dispensing charity to the less fortunate. As dame, madame, Madonna, in the old days of aristocracy, she bore equal rank with the lord and master, and carried down to our better democratic age the co-partnership of civic and family rights and duties.

Modern science and invention, civic and economic progress, the growth of humanitarian ideas, and the approach to Christian unity, are all combining to give woman and woman's work a central place in the social order. The vast machinery of government, especially in the new activities of the Agricultural and Labor departments applied to investigations and experiments into the questions of pure food, household economy, and employments suited to woman, is now directed more than ever before to the uplifting of American homes and the assistance of homemakers. These researches are at the call of every housewife. However, to save her the bewilderment of selection from so many useful suggestions, the fundamental principles of food and household economy as published by the government departments, are here presented, with the permission of the respective authorities, together with many other suggestions of utilitarian character which may assist the mother and housewife to a greater fulfillment of her office in the uplift of the home.

PRACTICAL
SUGGESTIONS
for
MOTHER
AND HOUSEWIFE

CHAPTER 1

THE SINGLE WOMAN

> She, keeping green
> Loves lilies for the one unseen,
> Counseling but her woman's heart,
> Chose in all ways the better part.
> BENJAMIN HATHAWAY—*By the Fireside.*

The question of celibacy is too large and complicated to be here discussed in its moral and sociological aspects. It is a condition that confronts us, must be accepted, and the best made of it. Whether by economic compulsion or personal preference, it is a fact that a large number of American men remain bachelors, and a corresponding number of American women content themselves with a life of "single blessedness." It is a tendency of modern life that marriage be deferred more and more to a later period of maturity. Accordingly the period of spinsterhood is an important one for consideration. It is a question of individual mental attitude whether the period be viewed by the single woman as a preparation for possible marriage, or as the determining of a permanent condition of life. In either case the problem before her is to choose, like Mr. Hathaway's heroine, "the better part."

The single woman has an advantage over her married sister in freedom of choice, of self-improvement, and service to others. Says George Eliot of the wife, "A woman's lot is made for her by the love she accepts." The "bachelor girl," on the other hand, has virtually all the liberty of the man whom her name indicates she emulates.

To the unmarried woman, especially the one who may subsequently marry, education in the broad sense of self-culture and development is of primary importance. The question of being should take precedence over doing, although not to the exclusion of the latter, for character is best formed by action. But all her studies, occupations, even her pastimes, should be pursued with the main purpose of making herself the ideal woman, such an one as Wordsworth describes, one with:

> "The reason firm, the temperate will,
> Endurance, foresight, strength and skill;
> A perfect Woman, nobly planned
> To warn, to comfort, and command;
> Any yet a Spirit still, and bright
> With something of angelic light."

It is an obviously true, and therefore a trite observation, that no one, woman or man, should consider that education (using the term broadly) stopped with graduation from school or college. But the statement that a grown person who has not settled down to some particular life work, such as is often the case with a young unmarried woman, should continue at least one serious *study*, will not be so generally accepted or acceptable. Yet in no other way may that mental discipline be obtained which is necessary to the mature development of character. Neglect to cultivate the ability to go down to the root of a subject, to observe it in its relations, and to apply it practically, will inevitably lead to superficial consideration of every subject, and even ignorance of the fact that this is superficial consideration. As a practical result, the person will drift through life rudderless, the sport of circumstance. She will act by impulse and chance, and be continually at a loss how to correct her errors. The shallowness with which women as a class are charged is due to the fact that, their aim in life for a considerable period not having been fixed by marriage or choice of a profession, they do not substitute some definite interest for such remissness, and so form the habit of intellectual laziness.

The study which an unmarried and unemployed woman should pursue may be anything worthy of thought, but preferably a practical subject at which, if necessary, the woman is ready to earn her living. Many a family has been saved from financial ruin by a daughter studying the business or profession of the father, and, upon his breakdown from ill-health, becoming his right-hand assistant, or, in the case of his death, even taking his place as the family bread-winner. In these days when farming is becoming more and more a question of the farmer's management, and less and less of his personal manual labor, a daughter in a farmer's family already supplied with one or more housekeepers may, as legitimately as a son, study the science of agriculture, or one of its many branches, such as poultry-raising or dairying, and with as certain a prospect of success. Ample literature of the most practical and authoritative nature on every phase of farming may be secured from the Department of Agriculture at Washington, and the various State universities offer special mid-winter courses in agriculture available for any one with a common-school education, as well as send lecturers to the farmer's institutes throughout the State.

To give examples of women who have made notable successes at farming and its allied industries would be invidious, since there are so many of them.

Studies that look to the possibility of the student becoming a teacher are preeminent in the development of mentality. The science of psychology is the foundation of the art of pedagogy, and every woman, particularly one who may some day be required to teach, should know the operations of the mind, how it receives, retains, and may best apply knowledge. An essential companion of this study is physiology, the science of the nature and functions of the bodily organs, together with its corollary, hygiene, the care of the health. From ancient times psychology and physiology have been considered as equally associated and of prime importance. "A sound mind in a sound body" is an old Latin proverb. The need of every one to "know himself," both in mind and body, was taught by the earliest "Wise Men" of Greece. The Roman emperor Tiberius said that any one who had reached the age of thirty in ignorance of his physical constitution was a fool, a thought that has been modernized, with an unnecessary extension of the age, into the proverb, "At forty a man is either a fool or a physician."

The study of psychology is a basis for every employment or activity which has to deal with enlightenment or persuasion of the public. The person who would like to become a speaker or writer needs to begin with it rather than with the study of elocution or rhetoric. The first thing essential for him to know is himself; the second, his hearers or readers—what is the order of progress in their enlightenment. Even logical development of a subject is subsidiary to the practical psychological order. Formal logic, the analysis of the process of reasoning, is a cultural study rather than a practical one, save in criticism both of one's own work and another's. More cultural, and at the same time more practical, is the study of exact reasoning in the form of some branch of mathematics. Abraham Lincoln, when he "rode the circuit" as a lawyer, carried with him a geometry, which he studied at every opportunity. To the mental training which it gave him was due his success not only as a lawyer, but also as a political orator. Every one of his speeches was a complete a demonstration of its theme as a proposition in Euclid is of its theorem. Lincoln once said that "demonstration" was the greatest word in the language.

Delineation of character is the chief element of fiction, and herein literary aspirants are particularly weak, especially the women, far more of whom than men try their hand at short stories and novels, and who are generally without that preliminary experience in journalism which most of the male writers have undergone. It is not enough for a novelist to "know life"; he must also know the literary aspect of life, must have the imaginative power to select and adapt actual experiences artistically. Young women who write are prone to record things "just as they happened." This is a mistake. Aristotle laid down the fundamental principle of creative work in his statement that the purpose of art is to fulfil the incomplete designs of nature—that is, aid nature by using her speech, yet telling her story the way she ought to have told it but did not. This is his great doctrine of "poetic justice."

The writing of children's stories is peculiarly the province of the woman author, and here, because of her knowledge of the mind of the child, she is apt to be most successful. The best of stories about children and for children have been written by school-teachers. Of these authors a notable instance was the late Myra Kelly, whose adaptations in story form of her experiences as a teacher to the foreign population of the "East Side" of New York will long remain as models of their kind.

Journalism is a sufficient field in itself for a woman writer in which to exercise her ability, as well as a preparation for creative literary work. The natural way to enter it is by becoming the local correspondent of one of the newspapers of the region. In this work good judgment in the choice of items of news, variety in the manner of stating them, and logical order in arranging and connecting them should be cultivated. The writing of good, plain English, rather than "smart" journalese should be the aim. Stale, vulgar and incorrect phrases, such as "Sundayed," and "in our midst," should be avoided. There are two tests in selecting a new item: (1) Will it interest readers? (2) Ought they to know it? When by these tests an item is proved to be real news that demands publication, it should be published regardless of a third consideration, which is too often made a primary one: Will it please the persons concerned? This consideration should have weight only in regard to the manner of its statement. When the news is disagreeable to the parties concerned, it should be told with all kindness and charity. Thus the facts of a crime should be stated, who was arrested for it, etc.; but there should be no positive statement of the guilt of the one arrested until this has been legally proved. Many a publisher has had to pay heavy damages because he has overlooked, or permitted to be published, an unwarranted statement or opinion of a reporter or correspondent. But even though there were no law against libel, the commandment against bearing false witness holds in ethics.

The woman at home may also become a contributor to the newspaper. Her first articles should be statements of fact on practical subjects, such as the result of her own or some neighbor's experiments in a household matter of general interest. Thus when a new church is erected, the history of the old one may be properly told. Here the amateur journalist may practise herself in interviewing people.

After such a preparation as this, one may confidently enter the active profession of journalism as a reporter, preferably upon the paper for which she has been writing. Since in entering any profession opportunity for improvement and advancement in it is the first consideration, the young reporter should cheerfully accept the low salary that is paid beginners. There is no discrimination on account of sex in the newspaper world. Copy is paid for according to its amount and quality, regardless of whether it was written by a woman or a man. Women labor here, as elsewhere, under physical disabilities in comparison with men, and yet in compensation they have the advantage over men in their special adaptation to certain features of newspaper work, such as the interviewing of women, writing household and fashion articles, etc. There are more chances for this kind of special work in large cities, and here the aspiring newspaper woman may go, when she has proved her ability.

Mrs. Ida Husted Harper, who stands in the front rank of newspaper women, has tersely stated the duties a woman reporter must undertake and the sacrifices she must make, as follows: "The woman who wishes to be a newspaper reporter should ask herself if she is able to toil from eight to fifteen hours of the day, seven days in the week; if she is willing to take whatever assignment may be given; to go wherever sent, to accomplish what she is delegated to do, at whatever risk, or rebuff, or inconvenience; to brave all kinds of weather; to give up the frivolities of dress that women love and confine herself to a plain serviceable suit; to renounce practically the pleasures of social life; to put her relations to others on a business basis; to subordinate personal desires and eliminate the 'ego'; to be careful always to disarm prejudice against and create an impression favorable to women in this occupation; to expect no favors on account of sex; to submit her work to the same standard by which a man's is judged."

The salaries earned by women as reporters are, with a few notable exceptions, not large. As low as $8 and $10 a week are paid to beginners; from $15 to $25 a week is considered a fair salary, and $30 a week an exceptionally good one for a woman who has not received recognition as a thoroughly experienced reporter.

It is from the ranks of newspaper women who have gone to the large cities and made a name for themselves as capable reporters that the editorial staffs of the magazines are recruited. As a rule they obtain their introductions by magazine contributions chiefly of special articles on subjects in which they have made themselves experts. The salaries of these positions range from $25 a week for assistant editors to $50 and upward for the heads of departments.

Book publishers employ women of this class to edit and compile works upon their specialties. Quite a number of women in New York earn several thousand dollars a year each at such work, while continuing their regular editorial labors.

Many newspaper women drift naturally into advertising writing, which is well-paid for when cleverly done. Since the goods chiefly advertised are largely for women, women have the preference as writers of advertisements. Then, too, manufacturers and advertising agents pay well for ideas useful in promoting the commodities of themselves or their clients. Here the woman at home may find out whether she has special ability as an advertising writer, by thinking out new and catchy ideas for the promotion of articles which she sees are widely advertised, and mailing these to the manufacturers. It is well if she have artistic ability, so that she may make designs of the ideas, though this is not essential.

It is the advertising columns of the newspapers and magazines, even more than the reading matter, which give a demand for work in illustration. To the woman who has talent rather than genius in drawing, illustration and commercial art afford a far safer field, in respect to remuneration, than the making of oil-paintings and water-colors. If ability in drawing in conjoined with ability in designing and writing advertisements, the earnings are more than doubled. Since payment for the individual drawing is more customary than employing an artist at a fixed salary, illustrating and the designing of advertisements can be done at home. There are many young girls just out of art-school who earn from $25 to $50 a week by such "piece-work."

Akin to this work is the designing of book-covers, for which publishers pay $15 to $25 each.

Of a more mechanical nature is making the drawings for commercial catalogues, and the prices paid are low, $9 a week being the rule for beginners. Designers of patterns, etc., for various manufacturers receive a similar amount at first. They may hope, after several years of experience, to rise to $25 a week, or possibly $30 or $35.

CHAPTER II

THE SINGLE WOMAN

Teaching is a profession that is particularly the province of the unmarried woman. The best teachers are those who have chosen it as their life-work, and have therefore thoroughly prepared themselves for it. A girl who takes a school position merely for the money that there is in it, expecting to give it up in a year or so, when she hopes to marry, is inflicting a grievous wrong on the children under her charge. There are other remunerative employments where her lack of serious intention will not be productive of lasting injury. Lack of preparation for teaching generally goes with this lack of intention, doubling the injury. Against this the examination for the school certificate is not always a sufficient safeguard, since many girls are clever enough to "cram up" sufficiently to pass the examination who have not had the perseverance necessary to master the subjects they are to teach, not to speak of that interest in the broad subject of pedagogy, without which the application of its principles in teaching the various branches to be neglected. Enthusiasm in her profession, a whole-hearted interest in each pupil as an individual personality should characterize every teacher, for next to the mother, she plays the most important part in the development of the coming generation.

There is a general complaint that the salaries of school-teachers are too low, measured by the rewards of persons of corresponding ability in other professions. When, however, the certainty of pay and the virtual assurance that the employment is for life if good service is rendered, are considered, together with the respect accorded the teacher by the community and the fact that her work necessarily tends to the cultivation of her mind, the lot of the school-teacher must be reckoned as one of the most favored. Americans are more prone than any other people to spend money on education, and this spirit is ever increasing, so that the school-teacher is more certain than the member of any other profession that she will be rewarded worthily in the future. The establishment of the Carnegie pension fund for retired college professors is an indication of this growing spirit, as well as the recent advance of the salaries of public school teachers in New York City and elsewhere, in recognition of the increase in the cost of living.

To the bright woman who is interested in the study of civics, political economy, and sociology, there is opportunity to earn a living at home by organizing classes in these subjects among the club-women of her town. Teachers of parliamentary law are in especial demand. The organization of a mock congress for parliamentary practise is the most entertaining as well as the most improving play in which women can join. There is also a demand among women who seek an intellectual element in their recreation for instruction in the games of bridge-whist, whist, and chess. Bridge-whist is the most popular, largely because of the desire to win money and valuable prizes at the game.

Then, too, a greater amount of time is spent at it than is legitimate for recreation. For moral reasons, therefore, the teaching of it cannot be recommended. Straight whist is also played occasionally for money, but this practise, happily, is rapidly becoming obsolete. Chess, except among professionals, is played purely for sport, and is therefore the best of games to study. Unfortunately there is very little demand for instruction in it by women; nevertheless, it is the best of all games for cultivating the analytical power of the mind, a faculty in which women, as a rule, are weak.

This power may, with equal pleasure and greater profit, be gained by paying special attention, in the reading of books and magazines, to literary style and construction. The average reader assimilates only a small percentage of what he reads. The careful thought which the author puts into his manner of presentation, no less than into the matter, is appreciated by very few of his readers, and by these only to a limited extent. Especially is this true of fiction. If one wishes to become an author, he should first cultivate this power of criticism, always accompanying the study by exercises in reconstruction of faults in the author read. Thus, wherever a

sentence appears awkward in expression, the
reader should revise it; wherever there is a
seeming error in the logical development of
a subject, or the psychological development
of a fictitious character, he should reconstruct
it. Nothing is so helpful to a writer as self-
criticism. Thus Mrs. Humphrey Ward has
recently confessed that the happy ending of her
"Lady Rose's Daughter" was an artistic error,
false to psychology, her heroine being doomed
to unhappiness by her character. After creating
his characters, and placing them in situations
where their individuality has proper scope for
action, the author must let them work out their
salvation. A thoroughly artistic work is marked
throughout by the quality of "the inevitable,"
and for this the reader should always be seeking. There is no surer indication of shallowness
than the desire to read only about pleasant subjects and characters and events. It is akin to the
habit of ignoring the existence of everything
disagreeable in life, which Dickens has satirized
in his character, Mr. Podsnap. And "Podsnap-
pery" exists among women even more than
among men, because of their more sensitive
emotional nature. If women are to join with
men in making the world better, they must not

blink at the misery and vice about them, and the evil elements in human nature and society which produce these. To be good and brave is better for a grown woman than to be "sweet" and "innocent," in the limited sense of these terms. A woman, like a man, should "see life steadily, and see it whole."

The foundation of a critical habit in reading has a practical bearing, inasmuch as it is a direct training for the positions of book-reviewer and manuscript reader for magazine and book publishers. Since women read more than men, the woman's view of a manuscript is often preferred by publishers. Therefore there are more women than men in the position of literary adviser. These are paid salaries ranging from $25 to $50 a week. Manuscripts are ready by the piece for from $3 to $5 each. Book reviews are paid for at all prices, from the possession of the book alone to the payment of a cent a word. It is best for the aspiring critic to practice herself on book reviews first. In these she can with profit display her power to analyze the artistic construction on books, and so develop her abilities as a manuscript reader.

The knowledge of books and the ability to digest their contents are necessary to the making of a library worker, an employment which the great increase in libraries, through the benefaction of Andrew Carnegie and others, is offering to thousands of American women. The salaries are low, but in considering entering upon the work, weight should be given to the opportunities for literary knowledge and culture it affords and its refined surroundings. The making of a descriptive catalogue of the home library, using the card index system, forms an ideal test for the young woman who is uncertain whether she has the taste and ability required in this sort of work. To the student in the home, even though she intends to follow some other vocation, such as teaching or writing, such an inventory of her intellectual store-house will be invaluable. It matters not how small the library is, for "intensive cultivation" is as profitable in mental culture as in agriculture.

Even such accomplishments as music and painting are most cultural when pursued as if the intention of the student were to teach them. Knowledge of technique and of the methods by which its difficulties are overcome is the foundation of all appreciation of art. The only true connoisseur is the one who can enter into the delight felt by the artist in creating his work. Exercise leads to invention. The ancients well said that the contortions of the sibyl generated her inspiration. Critics have been sneeringly defined as "those who have failed in literature in art," but this is not true of the greatest critics, who never carried their creative work to the point of success simply because they had found a better vocation in criticism before reaching such a point. What a loss to the world it would have been had Ruskin developed into a painter, even a great one, instead of the master interpreter and teacher of painting that he did become!

Household employments, such as cooking, needlework, etc., as vocations for the unmarried woman, no less than the married, need only be mentioned here, as their appropriateness for the girl at home is obvious, and they are fully discussed elsewhere in this series. It should be suggested, however, that the great leisure of the unmarried woman enables her to try experiments in these subjects while the married housewife is too fully occupied by the routine of her duties to undertake them. Indeed, if a woman become a notable cook after marriage, it is often a sign that she is not a notable wife or mother.

It is an old saying that,

> "My son's my son till he gets him a wife,
> But my daughter's my daughter all her life."

By the common bond of sex, a daughter is her mother's natural companion in sympathy, however separated from her in distance. Therefore, when she lives at home, what a special obligation is there to be her mother's comfort and dependence! Even though she acquire greater skill in household affairs, she should still resign herself to the subordinate place of assistant.

The thought that she is becoming useless is the chief dread of a woman who has been a managing worker all her life, and her daughter should carefully avoid bringing this to her mind, indeed, should so act that the ageing mother retains the management of the house, even though her labors diminish. In respect to the direction of children, the elder daughter should take a hint from the manner in which the school-teacher supplements rather than supplants the mother in her care of the young people, leading to a difference in the kind of regard which these feel for them. The sister should always consider herself simply as the eldest, most experienced of the children, and so the natural monitor of the group, and, when necessary, the mediator with the parents.

In a similar fashion the unmarried woman should act toward her neighbors who are wives and mothers. In matters where the interests of the children and households are of chief concern she should resign the leadership to the married women, and, after them, to the professional teachers. Religious, social, and civic matters, wherein as a church member and a citizen she is on an equal footing with wives and teachers, afford her ample scope for exercising her instinct for leadership.

Every unmarried woman who lives alone should, whether or not she possess an income, have a vocation. Earnings and wages are not alone good in themselves, but are an additional gratification, in that they supply a proof that the earner's service is of worth to the world. Some day, when social conditions are so adjusted that the economic conditions are so adjusted that economic competition is really free, and wealth cannot be obtained save by service, money will be a proper measure of standing in the community. It is all the more a duty now, both to herself, her class, and to society, that the woman who works should content to the last cent for her part of the wealth that is created by the business in which she is engaged. Where her work is equal to a man's she should contend for wages equal to his; where it is inferior, she should be willing to accept less; where superior, she should demand more. In these matters women are apt to be either too complaisant or too clamorous. They should first be sure that they are justified in their claims, and then, if right, be firm in their demands, and, if wrong, be resigned to abandon them. The law of supply and demand acting in the labor market allots wages between workers with natural justice—certainly more equitably than the interested opinion either of employer or employee.

It will be seen that the woman in business needs to study the fundamental elements of political economy even more than the housewife. Books and magazines are filled with superficial, obvious advice as to the way in which women as employees should conduct themselves toward their employers and fellow workers, but rarely is there a hint given of the actual rights and obligations of these relations, upon which the proper conduct is based.

Employment is a business contract between employer and employee, in which there is no legal or moral obligation for either party to exceed the terms. Owing to an over-supply of labor, wages may be exceedingly low, even down to the starvation point, but for this condition the employer, if he be not also a monopolist, is not responsible. Indeed, as employer, his presence in the labor market as an element of demand raises the market wage. In fact, it is only by his increasing his business that he can raise wages. If he pay more to his employees than he needs to, or is profitable for him, this increase is not real wages, but a gratuity, something no self-respecting person likes to take. Some other class in society created this condition, and it is this class that the low-paid workers should blame, and, as citizens, take measures against, not the employers. Indeed, they should consider these as their natural allies in making better economic conditions.

Accordingly, the woman in business should have sympathy for her employer, who owing to the prevalent condition of shackled competition has troubles of his own. She should aid him by loyal, efficient work, thus, and only thus, establishing a moral claim upon him to recognize her loyalty in kind. Personal relations, except of this nature, should not be sought by the employee, particularly if she is a woman. Outside of the office or shop she may meet and treat her employer as a fellow citizen and member of society, under the common rights of citizenship and the proper social rules, but in business hours she should obey the strict ethics of business. Thus she may don what dress she will when her work is done, adopt all the eccentricities of fashion she pleases, but she should wear with cheerfulness, and even pride, the simple dress prescribed, for good and sufficient reasons, as her working costume. Even when no such regulations are made, her good sense and taste should lead her to adopt a modest, practical working dress, simple mode of arranging the hair, etc. This is always agreeable to customers, and it is by pleasing these she best pleases her employer.

Stenographers and secretaries have a special obligation to keep sacred the confidences of their employers. If they find that in so doing they are made instruments in perpetrating frauds on other business men, or the community in general, they have no right to expose these. Their only proper course is to resign their positions, holding sacred, however, the knowledge gained while acting as employees. It is only when formally relieved of this obligation by legal compulsion to testify in court that they may reveal this knowledge.

While it is the custom of an employer to demand references of the employee, and not give them for himself, the only safe course for a woman seeking employment is to look into the character of the man for whom she is to work, and the nature of his business. If the employer refuses to impart this, saying, "Your work will be to do whatever I ask you," it is a blind, and therefore dangerous contract into which you are entering, and you should withdraw from it in time.

When an employee has proved her efficiency, and has seen that it is producing an amount of returns to the business of which she is not receiving her proportionate share, it is her right and duty to ask for an increase in wages. If she fails to receive this, she should investigate the conditions of the labor market of her class, and guide her action accordingly. If she finds that there is a demand for workers of her ability at the higher wage, she should again proffer her request to her employer, with a statement of this fact. If he still refuses the increase, she should resign her position, upon proper notice, and seek employment elsewhere.

When the unmarried woman employs herself in free service for the public good there will be no need for her to contend for the proper returns, which will be the love and respect of the community, given her in full measure. In comparison with these rewards, the honors of club president and society leader, for which many women contend with a rivalry that surpasses in bitterness contests for political honors among men, are mean and empty. The words of the Master to His disciples, that he who would be first among them should be servant to his fellows, should be taken to heart by American women, before whom are opening new and vast opportunities for the display of pride and ambition no less than for modest, faithful service.

CHAPTER III

THE WIFE

Nature's Intention in Marriage—The Woman's Crime in Marrying for Support—Her Blunder in Marrying an Inefficient Man for Love—The Proper Union—Mutual Aid of Husband and Wife—Manipulating a Husband—By Deceit—By Tact—Confidence Between Man and Wife.

> "Her very soul is in home, and in the discharge of all those quiet virtues of which home is the centre. Her husband will be to her the object of all her care, solicitude and affection. She will see nothing but by him, and through him. If he is a man of sense and virtue, she will sympathize in his sorrows, divert his fatigue, and share his pleasures. If she becomes the property of a churlish or negligent husband, she will suit his taste also, for she will not long survive his unkindness."
>
> SIR WALTER SCOTT—*Waverley.*

Marriage is the crown of woman's life, a dignity that is all the more honorable because it is of general expectation and realization. There is a presumption that the unmarried woman has missed the central and significant reason for her existence, the perpetuation and nurture of the race, and that the burden is upon her for compensating society by other services for this lost opportunity. Marriage for a woman means attainment first and fulfillment after, the reward given in advance of labor, and therefore entailing a special moral obligation that it be justified in its fruits. Nature gives the future mother peace of mind, rest from doubt as to career and from responsibility as to breadwinning, in order that she may tranquilly devote herself to her special function as the maker of the home.

The fact that in the normal home the wife is relieved from the necessity of earning the living of the home sometimes has the effect of making her careless about expenditure. The thoughtless wife, and here thoughtless means selfish, assumes that the problem of providing is "up to" the husband and takes no care to aid him in its solution. If the suggestion of her being a burden to him ever does cross her mind, she is ready to excuse herself by consolatory sayings such as "Two can live cheaper than one," the truth of which, though universal when every wife was a producer of such things as clothing that are now bought, is now the case only in agricultural homes, and even there has lost a great deal of force. Men do not marry now, as they once did, for economic reasons, but rather in spite of them, for the higher rewards of love and companionship of wife and children, and this the wife should recognize by giving her husband the things for which he has made his economic sacrifice. In the old days a man who did not marry paid for his liberty by loss of physical comfort and wealth. Thus Hesiod, one of the earliest Greek poets, in his Farmer's Almanac called "Works and Days," coupled the marrying of a wife with the purchase of a yoke of oxen and a plow as the first things needful in beginning to farm, and this in despite of the fact that he was a woman-hater.

Now it is the woman who is tempted to marry for economic reasons, to be certain of material support while she exercises herself in those household avocations and social pleasures which constitute the main activities of women. This is a legitimate consideration only when the interest of the man is also taken into account. Marriage to a man whom she does not love is a crime for any woman; giving falsely the offerings of love for material things is harlotry even though legitimated by vows and ceremonies.

On the other hand, marriage for love to a man who cannot support her is a sad mistake for a woman who is not able or willing to take the place of breadwinner, for such a union defeats its own purpose. Therefore, in kindness to the man as well as to herself, such a woman should satisfy herself that he can support her, not necessarily in "the style to which she has been accustomed," but in the style necessary for her to perform the duties of homemaker and mother. Those marriages are the happiest where a wife can also enter into sympathy with her husband's business ambitions in particular and ideals of life in general. Here she is peculiarly his helpmate. He can hire a housekeeper, but not a companion of his bosom.

A girl properly reared will naturally be drawn to a man complementary to her in character— not "opposite," as is so often said. Opposition implies antagonism, which would be the ruin of home life. The term complementary implies similarity in the main elements of character with adaptable differences. Good qualities, such as strength and delicacy, may complement each other, but not evil and good qualities, such as brutality and tenderness. As Scott says in the quotation at the head of this chapter, a tender wife may suit the taste of a churlish husband, but only by not long surviving his unkindness. While such opposition may not result in actual death, it certainly leads to the demise of all that makes life worth living.

A woman should not expect to find a perfect husband. Indeed, her chief usefulness to him will be in her strengthening his weak points, and cultivating his right inclinations until they are confirmed habits. Yet in this work she should realize the imperfections of herself, and respond to the similar aid he gives her by his example and suggestions. Mutual aid is the great bond of marriage, as it is of all human relations.

Women, from their weaker condition, have from ages past been trained to gain their desires from men by indirection. In the worst form, this appears as deceit; in the best, as tact. Laying aside the moral aspect, deceit is always unwise in a wife, since, in time, it defeats its own end. Many a woman thinks that she is deceiving her husband, since she wins her points, when he thoroughly recognizes her machinations, and accedes to them without contest simply for peace in the household, acquiring a feeling of moral superiority to her which, though it may be tolerant, is nevertheless contemptuous. But when she employs loving tact, especially in the improvement of her husband's habits and traits, even though he realizes it, he is at heart grateful for it, and proud of his wife's superiority in these points.

In those matters where the characters of husband and wife are strong enough to permit frankness, this should always be employed. In all the grave problems of life there should be perfect confidence between the pair who have taken the solemn vows of wedlock. Any third party that enjoys superior confidence with one of them, whether relative or friend, even the pastor or family physician, is the man invoked against in the marriage charge, who "puts them asunder." Where unhappily the husband is irreligious and the wife is forced to seek confidential help and consolation of her spiritual adviser, she should strictly limit these to religious matters, else she will grow apart from her husband. George Moore, in his collection of stories entitled, "The Untilled Field," presents the propensity of women in Ireland to run to the priest for guidance on every question, as the chief cause of their domestic tragedies. In America the family physician is as apt as the pastor to be made the recipient of such confidences, with evil results where he is not wise enough to advise that the husband is the proper person to whom the wife should go.

CHAPTER IV

THE HOUSE

> Of love, of joy, of peace and plenty: where,
> Supporting and supported, polished friends
> And dear relations mingle into bliss.
> JAMES THOMSON—*The Seasons.*

When husband and wife are truly mated, they form a co-partnership in the building of the home. In this work the man, occupied with his business, must leave a large part of the direction, even in material things, to the woman. And these material things are of primary consideration, as they are apt to be in every problem of life. The happiness of home is immediately and always dependent on the kind of a house used for dwelling and its equipment for utility and comfort.

The first thing to be considered is the location of the home. The choice of a good neighborhood, from both social and sanitary viewpoints, is essential. Good neighbors are almost as necessary as good air and good drainage. Even before the children have come, it is a limitation on the function of a home for husband and wife to be forced to seek social life entirely outside the neighborhood. If charity (that is, loving, helpful associations) begins at home, it certainly does not stop at the threshold, or leap therefrom over those nearest to us. The best citizens are those who take a human interest in the people of their street, or ward, or village, for influence in civic reform is dependent on neighborliness.

Children are good citizens in this respect by nature. Limited to association with children of the neighborhood, they form an affection for their playmates, which may lead to good or evil results, as these playmates are moral or vicious in their tendencies. Therefore, at the formative period of character children should be guarded from the debasing influences of improper companions, as well as such institutions as saloons and low dancehalls which are generally found to be the local causes of bad neighbors.

Of course, a neighborhood should be selected where there are good public schools, churches, and allied institutions for education and culture. It is always a loss to a child in this democratic country to be educated in a private school, and yet, especially in cities, careful parents are often compelled to resort to private instruction for their girls and boys because of the lack of refining influences in the public schools. This is why it is often better for families, when the father works in the city, to live in the suburbs, where, as a rule, the best public schools are to be found.

But it may not be feasible to live out of the city, especially in the first years of married life, and therefore the home life must begin in an apartment. The same sanitary considerations that obtain in choice of a neighborhood are essential in the choice of a flat. Good air, light, space, proper plumbing, and general cleanness are to be sought. Owing to the general demand for these advantages, and a limited supply of them which is due to economic conditions prevailing in our cities, they unfortunately require money, therefore, the flat-seeker is compelled to do the best he can with that part of his income which he may safely appropriate for rent. As a rule, this amount is not more than one-fourth of income.

When an apartment house has been properly built, and the walls are settled and the plastering dry, it generally comes up to the standard of comfort and health. Here the latest improvements in plumbing will be apt to be found, and there will be no danger of vermin. Then, too, a concession is more apt to be made by the landlord, who is anxious to secure tenants, by remission of a month's or a fortnight's rent, to be taken out after the first month. The landlord of such a house is also readier than the owner of an old one to make decorations, and even alterations, to suit the taste of the tenant.

The walls in the kitchen should be painted rather than papered, and other parts of the flat designed primarily for utility. Since light is the great desideratum, the paint, as a rule, should be light in color, though soft and tinted in tone for restfulness to the eye. Where wallpaper is used, it should have the same characteristics. Fanciful designs should be avoided. Indeed, plain paper forms the best base for artistic color schemes in the decoration of rooms, the variety in which is best obtained by the choice of furniture and pictures and other wall ornaments.

When there is a prospect that living in apartments will be only a temporary arrangement, the furniture should be chosen with a view to its adaptability for a house. Thus folding-beds should be avoided, and other articles that gain space by complexity, however ingenious. Simplicity is the quality to be desired. Thus if the exigency of space requires that a living room by day be converted into a sleeping room, a couch should be bought for it, instead of a folding bed. It will then serve the purpose of a sofa as well as a bed. If it is a box couch, further economy will be gained by its use as a place to store the bedclothes. But the simplest of all arrangements is a divan bed, formed of springs and mattress alone, and supported on legs nailed to the corners of the spring-frame. Over it a cover should be thrown during the day, and the pillows in use, if there is not room for them elsewhere, should be slipped into covers harmonious in color with the couch drapery. Such a reclining and sleeping couch may also be used in bedrooms, although an iron or brass bedstead gives an appearance of neatness and personal privacy that is desirable in such chambers.

Where there is lack of closet space and lockers, trunks can be utilized in a flat for storing things. Steamer trunks that can be placed beneath the beds and couches are therefore the best kind to buy. They can also be readily converted into window seats by making pads of cotton batting to fit the tops, and placing over them covers and pillow cushions harmonious with the decoration of the room. Long flat "wardrobe trunks" are sold, which contain at one end rods for hanging clothes, so that, when stood up on the other end against the wall they serve as wardrobes. They always look, however, like makeshifts, and so are more useful in traveling than in the home.

Rugs are more desirable than carpets in a city apartment, since they can be more readily cleaned, and, in case of moving to another flat or a house in the suburbs, will more adaptable to the new situation.

Bookcases in a temporary home should be of the unit system, where each shelf is a separate box enabling the books to be moved without repacking, and permitting rearrangement to suit the new situation, or the acquisition of new books. Where, however, the lower part of wall space is desired to give room for articles of furniture such as couches, shelves can be built, beginning at four and one-half or five feet above the floor. Mr. Edwin Markham, the poet, whose home overflows with books, has greatly economized space by building for them a broad lower shelf, about eighteen inches wide, and, three inches above this, another shelf twelve inches wide, and three inches about this, a third six inches wide. When these are filled with books the titles of all are exposed, and, by taking out the volume or two immediately in front, a volume on one of the back shelves is readily obtained. Thus, by walking about his room, Mr. Markham can look with level eyes for the book he wants, and procure it without recourse to a chair or stepladder. This plan of banking books also lends itself to an arrangement of them.

Except in matters such as these, where economy is imperative, the furnishing of a city apartment does not differ essentially from that of a house, and the reader is therefore referred to the discussion of this in the following pages.

The suburban, village, or country home differs from the city apartment, or even city house, in that it has been built without the primary consideration of space. It is separated from other houses, even though by the narrowest space of green lawn, that gives a

house the individuality and independence without which it is hard for it to gather the
associations of home. Even when a detached
house is found in a city, its architecture is generally hampered by its adaptation to its narrow
grounds. It rarely has that rounded development of character which is as desirable in a
home as in a person.

In selecting a rented home in the suburbs,
the cost of the husband's transportation to and
from the city should be added to the rent to
keep this within the proper ratio to income,
just as the difference in the price of provisions
should be considered in that portion allotted to
food. Provisions, even country produce, are
often dearer in suburban communities than in
the city, and less saving can be made by close
marketing, because the farmers and gardeners
find it more profitable to send their produce to
the center of greatest demand, and therefore of
readiest sale, even though it costs more for
transportation than to the smaller markets near
by. So suburban grocers and provision men are
wont to buy in the city markets, and add the
cost of transportation back from the city, and
an additional profit for the transaction, to the
price to the consumer.

Owing to the close competition for house-holders among real-estate men, it is now almost as easy to purchase a suburban home as it is to rent one, and it is therefore advisable to do this. The interest on purchase, and the fixed charges of taxes, insurance, water rent, etc., should be counted as rent, but a higher percentage of income may be safely allotted to these than to rent proper, since the purchase is also an investment. As a rule, the increase of land value near a growing city will considerably exceed the diminution in the value of the improvements. Indeed, owing the constant advance of cost of building material in recent years, there is often enhancement rather than depreciation in the house value.

For these economic reasons it is advisable to buy an old house when its cost is less than the cost of constructing a new one of the same desirability. The home-seeker, however, should curb his propensity to make extensive alterations, for, one leading to another, he will find at the end (if he ever reaches it) that he has virtually built a new house at a cost greater than he could afford.

On the other hand, he should avoid those houses built on speculation to sell. In these a showy appearance is gained at the expense of durability of construction, and the purchaser will find that he must pay in plumbing, coal bills, and general repairs an amount he had not calculated upon as interest on the home, for, unless he rebuilds the house at ruinous expense, these will be annual charges.

The most satisfactory way, and the one leading to great enjoyment in satisfying the "nest-building" instinct which possesses newly mated people no less than birds, is for the owners themselves to plan and superintend the building of the home. There is an infinite variety of architectural plans spread before the home-seeker in books and magazines. An examination of these will be of great value to him in clarifying his hazy ideas, but he should not settle upon any one of them without expert opinion. He should employ a local architect, or at least a builder with practical architectural ideas, to examine every feature of the plan selected as nearest the homeseeker's ideal, and revise it accordingly to local conditions, cost and availability of material, etc. Money is always well spent that relieves one of responsibility, enabling him to say thereafter, "Well, I did everything I could to have the thing done properly."

The woman's wish should be paramount in planning the building. The home is her workshop, and she should have every convenience she requires to do her work properly. Things that appear of minor importance to a man, the architect and builder no less than her husband, are to her most vital. What pockets are to a man or business woman in clothes, closets and shelves are to a woman in her house, and yet she usually has to fight for them with the architect as the business woman does for pockets with her dressmaker. Unless she has worked out the practicability of her ideas, however, she will be at a great disadvantage with the experts, and therefore it is wise for her to make herself as familiar as possible with the main principles of building and the special details of the improvements she desires, especially as this knowledge will be of great use in seeing that the work is done as ordered. Where she has not acquired this knowledge, and the husband is either incompetent or not free to undertake this supervision, it is well to employ a contractor, arranging for thorough, satisfactory work, and holding him strictly to the contract.

The prime requisite in a house is that it be adapted for home life, be a comfortable place in which to sleep, cook, eat, rest and read, talk and laugh, and play and pray; in a word, in which to do all the work that enables these necessities and pleasures to be obtained. Next to the comfort of the family comes that of the outside world. It is desirable, though not essential, that the home contain facilities for entertaining.

CHAPTER V

THE HOUSE

Essential Parts of a House—Double Use of Rooms—
Utility of Piazzas—Landscape Gardening—Water-
supply—Waterpower—Illumination—Dangers from
Gas—How to Read a Gas-meter—How to Test
Kerosene—Care of Lamps—Use of Candles—Mak-
ing the Best of the Old House.

The parts that are desirable in a well-ordered
house may be enumerated as follows: Cellar, the
kitchen, the storehouse, the pantry, the laundry,
the dining-room, the living or sitting-room,
the lavatory, the parlor, the hall, the library,
the nursery, the sewing-room, the bedrooms,
including guest chamber, the attic, the piazzas.

Where economy of space must be practiced,
storehouse and pantry may be combined, and
nursery and sewing-room; and one of the family bedrooms may be devoted to the use of the
occasional guest. The hall may be thrown into
the parlor. The parlor may be properly converted into a library and music room, although
when the father is of retiring literary tastes, he

should have a "den" of his own, where he may read and smoke in peace.

The parlor is too often wasted space in a house. As the "best room," and very often the largest room, it is reserved for reception of guests, weddings, and funerals, and at other times shut up in gloomy grandeur from the family, except, perhaps, as the place of banishment for a naughty child. Except when used as a library and music room, it should be one of the smallest in the house, and may, indeed, be entirely dispensed with. The family living-room is not an improper place in which to receive a guest, especially one whom it is desired should "feel at home."

Of the rooms for the family, the nursery is the best to dispense with, the very young children being kept under the mother's oversight in her sewing-room, or the attic, or a loft in an out-building being fitted up for the elder ones as a play-room. In the case of the loft, it is well to equip it as a simple gymnasium.

It is mistaken economy to use the living-room as a dining-room, since this interferes with the orderly work of the house, no less than with the comfort of the family. It may with propriety, however, be made also the sewing-room, and, in general, the mother's managerial office. Here she should keep her desk and her household account-books, and meet the tradesmen and other business callers. It is also more suited than the parlor for use as a family reading-room and working library. Disorder that betokens use, such as magazines on the center-table, or of papers on the desk, is here not inappropriate. Indeed, it gives a home-like appearance even to the social guest.

China and glassware and silver arranged in proper array in wall closets, cabinets, and sideboards are the most appropriate decorations of the dining-room. It is not at all necessary that there should be pictures on the wall of game, fruit and flowers, or "still life" studies of vegetables and kitchen utensils. Indeed, these have become so expected that a change is quite a relief to a guest, who would welcome even the death's head that was the invariable ornament of the Egyptian feasts. Any pictures which are lively and cheerful in suggestion are suitable. Those that have a story to tell or a lesson to point are never out of place in a room frequented by children.

For convenience the table-linen should be kept in drawers or lockers built beneath the shelves containing the china. A butler's pantry is not an essential when such arrangements as these are made.

The kitchen, pantry, storeroom, and laundry form, as it were, the "factory" of the house, with the range as the central "engine." Accordingly they should be planned with respect to each other to save steps. Fortunately this means also saving expense in construction. Architects have been most ingenious as well as practical in perfecting these arrangements, and the house-builder, therefore, needs no advice from us.

It cannot be too much emphasized, however, that the cellar is, from the standpoints of sanitation and comfort, the most important part of the house. There should be no attempt to save expense by limiting its proper size, materials for walls, windows for ventilation, drainage, etc., for money so saved will inevitably be paid out many times over in coal bills, doctor's fees, and, perhaps, undertaker's bills. A dry cellar must be secured at all costs, for the air from it permeates the whole house. Where this is damp, it leads not alone to disease among the inmates, but to the disintegration of the house itself, through what is called "dry rot," but is paradoxically the result of dampness. Edgar Allan Poe, in his weird story, "The Fall of the House of Usher," has given a mystical interpretation of the dissolution of an old homestead which really has a scientific explanation that might be found in the cellar.

The proper floor of a cellar is a layer of broken stones in which tile drains are laid, having outlets into a common drain, and over which a layer of concrete is placed. The walls, of plastered stone, brick, or concrete, should rise above the ground far enough to permit small windows and prevent the admission of surface water from rain or snow. These windows should open from within, upward, and there should be hooks on the ceiling to keep them open for ventilation.

Where a house is heated by a furnace, the style of this should be selected with great care, special regard being had to the economy of fuel. The systems of steam-heating, hot-water heating, or hot-air heating have each their merits, depending on the location of the house and the climate of the region. The cellar can also be used as a storeroom for those things not affected by the heat of the furnace, such as perishable food requiring an ice-box or a cool place, vegetables, especially those with a penetrating odor; apples, canned fruit and goods, etc., should be kept here, and barrels of commodities, such as vinegar, that are bought in large quantities. Shelves should be built on the walls and books hung on the rafters to increase the facilities for storage. Articles hung upon the hooks should be tied in paper bags. It is well to have the cellar ceiled, to keep out the dust of the house and reduce the risk of fire. Here, of course, is the natural place for the coal-bin, and, when there are no out-buildings, the man's workshop. The laundry may also be placed in the cellar, and in stormy weather, the clothes hung there to dry. In the country the cellar is a good place in which to build an ice-vault.

The kitchen should, of course, be airy and sunny. The sink should be placed near a south window, if possible, to prevent freezing of pipes. An iron sink is more cleanly than a wooden one, and cheaper than porcelain and copper. It should have a platform with room for two dishpans, and a drying shelf, raised at one end to permit drainage. Where economy of space is essential, this shelf may be removable, permitting the use for other things of the table beneath.

Two other tables are necessary in a proper kitchen equipment, one covered with zinc for a work-table, set near the range, and the other a plain table set near the dining-room, for the prepared dishes. There should be three lights, lamps in brackets, gas-jets, or electric bulbs, near the sink, range and food-table respectively. The refrigerator should be put outside the kitchen, in some such place as a sheltered part of the back piazza. Commodities such as tea and coffee, not requiring ice, should be kept in covered jars, preferably earthen, on a dresser or shelf, where the bread-box may also stand. There should be a kitchen closet for the flour-barrel and sugar-box, which should be covered for further protection from dust, flies, damp-ness, etc., and for the canned goods in immediate requisition.

The stove or range should be selected with reference on the one hand to the amount of cooking to be done for the family, and on the other to the saving of fuel. Where there is a water supply, of course there should be a boiler connected with the range. This should be large enough to assure a sufficient supply of hot water for the house. There should be a shelf near the range for such articles as the pepper-box and salt-box which are in constant use in cooking, and hooks should be near at hand for

hanging up the poker, lid-lifter, and a coarse
towel for use in taking pans from the oven.
Other shelves and hooks, of course, should be
put in for the various utensils necessary in the
kitchen.

The floor of the kitchen should be covered
with a good quality of linoleum. A perforated
rubber mat may be placed at the sink, although
this is not necessary. In fact, it is a better plan
for the woman in the kitchen, as indeed elsewhere, to get rubber heels for her shoes. The
Arabs have a proverb that to him who is shod
it is as if the whole world were covered with
leather, and rubber heels similarly cause every
floor in the house, whether bare or carpeted,
to be equally easy to the feet of the busy housewife.

The laundry should be supplied with two
tubs, an ironing-table, an ironing-board, and a
stove for the boiler and the irons. The ironing-
board should be supported upon two "horses"
of the height of the table. The table should be
supplied with an iron-rest.

In a well-planned house there should be separate bedrooms for every inmate except the
very small children. It is quite an economy in
the care of the house that each child, at as early

an age as possible, should have its own room and be taught to take care of it. Since the room is designed primarily for sleeping, care should be taken that the bed be placed in such a position that the light falls from behind the sleeper's head. The dresser should be so placed that the light falls on the face of the occupant of the room when he is looking into the mirror. Even at the expense of space in the bedroom proper, there should be a large closet in every sleeping-room. The deeper the closet the better, for, by using rods attached to the back of the closet and projecting through its width, whereon clothes-hangers may be strung, far more room will be obtained for clothes than where hooks and nails are employed. By the use of these clothes-hangers, too, suits and dresses may be kept in much better order. The top of the closet may be occupied by one broad, high shelf, whereon hats and bonnets may be kept in their proper receptacles. Shoes should be kept in a drawer at the bottom of the closet, rather than thrown on the floor beneath the dresser. It is a mistake to substitute a curtain for the door of the closet, since it is of the first importance to keep the clothing free from dust.

Shelves are better than closets for the keeping of the bed linen. It is a handy thing to have a separate linen closet in the house, but this is not essential. The sewing-room of the mother is a suitable place for keeping the linen. Shelves are preferable to closets for this purpose. There should also be a medicine closet or locker in the mother's room which will be handy in case of sudden illness among the children.

In view of the importance of sanitation, more thought than is ordinarily allotted to it should be given to the lavatory. Where there is room to spare, it is best to have the bath separate from the toilet, in order to prevent inconvenience in use. There should be a basin and toilet upon the ground floor, and a bathroom and toilet upon the sleeping floor. The walls of the lavatory should be tiled, or, if this is too expensive, they should be covered with water-proof paper. All toilet arrangements should be systematically kept clean, and the necessary supplies at all times provided.

Piazzas may be made to add no less to the utility than to the beauty and comfort of the house. A lower back piazza, covered with vines, is the ideal place in summer for eating and such heating labors as ironing. When thoroughly secured from intrusion, an upper balcony furnishes the best of sleeping quarters for one wise and brave enough to scout the superstition of the bad effects of night air. Many persons of delicate health, even consumptives, have been restored to vigorous strength by sleeping in such a place, not only in summer but throughout the winter, save in beating storms.

Closely conjoined with forethought for utility in the planning of a house is forethought for beauty. It is well to have an artistic imagination in visualizing, as it were, the "hominess" of the house as it will appear after its rawness has been mellowed by time, and its forms have been endeared by association. This imagination is specially essential in the planting of trees, arrangement of flower gardens, the choice of the kind of enclosure, whether hedge or fence, and, in general, all that is known under the name of landscape gardening.

The housekeeper's work is greatly dependent upon the kind of water supply available for the house. In cities and towns the kind of supply is fixed for her, but in the country she is afforded her freedom of choice. She has a choice of water from wells or springs, which is more or less "hard," that is, impregnated with lime, and water collected from rain or melting snow. For household purposes rainwater is the more desirable, and, when properly filtered and kept in clean cisterns protected from the larvae of mosquitoes and other disease-bearing insects, it is also the best for drinking purposes. To one accustomed to drinking hard water from a well or spring, rain water is a little unpalatable, but after he is accustomed to its use he will prefer it. It is always wise to secure an analysis of the drinking water of the house, since water reputed pure because of its clearness and coldness is as apt as any other to be contaminated. Where soft water is not available for household use, hard water may be softened by the addition to it of pearline or soda, or by boiling, in the latter case the lime in it being precipitated to the bottom of the kettle or boiler.

When well water is used for drinking some knowledge of the geology of the home grounds is essential. Thus, because the top of a well is on higher ground than the cess-pool is no reason for assuming that the contents of the latter may not seep into the water, for the inclination of the strata of the rocks may be in a contrary direction to that of the surface of the ground.

When filters and strainers are used they should be carefully cleaned at regular intervals, since if they are permitted to accumulate impurities they become a source of contamination instead of its remedy. Every once in a while the housekeeper should take off the strainers from the faucets and boil them.

There are many excellent systems for obtaining water power for the house in the country, each of which has its special advantages. The pumping of water to a tank at the top of the house by a windmill is that most commonly used. This is the cheapest method, but the most unsightly. Small kerosene or hot-air engines may be employed for the power at very slight cost, and will prove useful for other purposes, such as sawing wood or even operating the sewing-machines. Owing to the many inventions for isolated lighting plants by acetylene and other kinds of gas, dwellers in the country have virtually as free a choice of illumination as the people in towns and cities.

Great caution is necessary in the use of any form of illuminating gas, since all produce asphyxiation. Accordingly, all gas fixtures of the house should be regularly inspected to see that there is no escape of the subtile, destructive fluid. The odor of escaping gas which is so unpleasant is really a blessing, in that it informs the householder of his danger. A cock that turns completely around and, after extinguishing the light, permits the escape of the gas, is more dangerous than a poisonous serpent. Yet there may be nothing radically wrong with this fixture, and the use of the screwdriver may make it as good as new. Gas should never be turned low when there is a draught in the room, nor allowed to burn near hanging draperies. Care should always be taken in turning out a gas-stove or a drop-light to do so at the fixture and not at the burner. This is not alone safer, but it keeps the rubber tube from acquiring a disagreeable odor from the gas that has been left in it.

Great economy in the consumption of gas may be secured by the use of Weisbach an other incandescent burners. Where these are not employed, care should be taken to select the most economical kind of gas tips, and to see that when these become impaired by use they are replaced.

In the large cities there is constant complaint of defective gas-meters, so much so that inspectors have been appointed to correct this abuse.

It has been found, however, that many complaints have been unfounded because the housewives were not able properly to read the meter. Directions how to do this will therefore be found useful. A gas-meter has three dials marking up to 100,000 feet, 10,000 feet, and 1,000 feet respectively. The figures on the second dial are arranged in opposite order from those on the first and third dials, and this often leads to an error in reckoning. However, there should be no trouble in setting down the figures indicated by the pointer on each dial. We first set down the figure indicated upon the first dial in the units place of a period of three places, then that indicated upon the second dial in the tens place, and then that indicated upon the third dial in the hundreds place. To these we add two ciphers, to obtain the number of feet of gas that has been burned since the meter was set at zero on the three dials. From this number we subtract the total of feet burned at the time when the preceding gas bill was rendered. This is generally called on the bill "present state of meter." The result of the subtraction will be the amount of gas that has been burned since the last bill was rendered.

For example:

> 95,300, amount indicated on the dial.
> 82,700, amount marked "present state of
>   meter" on preceding gas bill.
>
> ———
>
> 12,600, amount of gas for which current
> bill is rendered.

Equal care must be exercised when kerosene is used for illumination, since, while it is not so dangerous directly to life, it is the chief source of the destruction of property. Accordingly the nature of kerosene and the way it illuminates is a profitable subject of study if we would prevent destructive fires. Really, we do not burn the oil, but the gas that arises from the oil when liberated by the burning wick and becomes incandescent when fed by the oxygen of the air. While kerosene requires a high temperature for combustion, it is closely related to other products of coal oil, such as naphtha and gasoline, which become inflammable at a low heat and are therefore very dangerous. Since the cheap grades of kerosene approach these products in quality, care should be taken to see that it is of high "proof" in order to prevent explosions. The proof required of kerosene differs in various States; that in some is as low as 100 degrees Fahrenheit, that is, the temperature at which the oil will give off vapors that will ignite. This is too low a proof, for such a degree of temperature is quite common in the household. It is safe only to use that kerosene which is at least 140 degrees proof, for then, even though the oil is spilled, there is little danger that it will ignite except in the immediate presence of flame. There is no danger at all in soaking wood with this kind of oil in a stove or grate wherein the fire has gone out.

To test kerosene, put a thermometer into a cup partially filled with cold water, and add boiling water until the mercury stands at 130 degrees Fahrenheit. Then take out the thermometer and pour two teaspoonfuls of kerosene into the cup and pass over it the flame of a candle. If the oil ignites, it is unsafe.

In order to prevent the flame from running down into the lamp and causing an explosion, the wick should be soft, filling the burner completely. The highest efficiency in the form of illumination is obtained by round burners especially those in lamps which admit air to the inside of the wick and so induce the largest possible amount of combustion. Such a lamp produces quite a high degree of heat, and will answer the purpose of an oil-stove in a small room.

Contrary to the popular idea, wicks should be carefully trimmed with scissors rather than with a match or other instrument. In extinguishing a lamp one should first turn down the wick and blow across the chimney, never down the chimney.

Owing to the fact that the wick is constantly bringing up oil by capillary attraction, whether it is lighted or unlighted, lamps in which the wicks have not been cared are kept continually greasy. In fact, a lamp that is greasy or that gives out a bad odor is one that has not been properly cared. With due attention, lamps are as clean and handy a means of illumination as any other form.

Candles, that are now used chiefly for decorative purposes, may still be practically employed for carrying light about the house. The danger from a falling candle carried by a child up to bed is not nearly so great as that which may result from either spilt oil from a broken lamp or the cutting glass of its chimney.

To those who live in an old house, all the foregoing advice should prove a source of helpfulness in making the best of the old home, rather than of dissatisfaction with its seeming shortcomings. There are many simple, inexpensive ways of making it conform to the model house. Expense need only be incurred in sanitary improvement, such as the better drainage of the cellar, enabling it to be utilized for purposes which now crowd the "workrooms" of the home, and the alterations of the windows to permit better lighting and ventilation. Very often a room can be made to exchange purposes by a simple transference of furniture, thus saving the housekeeper steps. A woodhouse can be converted into a summer kitchen, and the old one, during this season, used as a dining-room, though it may be found even pleasanter to eat out of doors under an arbor or on a wide piazza. A porch may be partitioned off into a laundry, and the attic ceiled and partitioned for use as a bedroom. Very often an old boxed-off stairway, built in the days when it was thought unseemly to show a connection with the upper bedrooms, can be relieved of its door and walls, to the increase of space in the lower room, and of the beauty of its appearance. Indeed, as a rule, there are too many doors in an old house. Some of these can be altered into open arched entrances, making one large commodious room out of two little inconvenient ones. Unused out-buildings can be turned into playrooms for the children, and even sleeping quarters. All these are changes that make for the beauty no less than the utility of home, as proved by the fact that may artists, especially those who have studies abroad where old country houses are more or less or this unconventional character, go into the country and alter in this fashion old and even abandoned houses into houses admired for their charming individuality. Illustrations of such "hermitages" frequently appear in the magazines, and may be studied for suggestions. Sometimes the alteration is of the exterior only. The repainting in a proper color or the simple creosote staining of a weather-beaten house, with the addition of a rustic porch or the breaking of a corner bedroom into a balcony, will sometimes so transform an old house that it looks as if it were a new creation.

CHAPTER VI

FURNITURE AND DECORATION

The Qualities to Be Sought in Furniture—Home-made Furniture—Semi-made Furniture—Good Furniture as an Investment—Furnishing and Decorating the Hall—The Staircase—The Parlor—Rugs and Carpets—Oriental Rugs—Floors—Treatment of Hardwood—Of Other Wood—How to Stain a Floor—Filling as a Floor Covering.

> Necessity invented stools,
> Convenience next suggested elbow-chairs,
> And Luxury the accomplished sofa last.
> WILLIAM COWPER— *The Task.*

Utility, comfort and elegance are, as Cowper shows, the three successive purposes for which furniture was designed. And to-day the order of development remains also the order of importance. The first things to be desired in any article of furniture are durability and simple application to its purpose. These being found, a person naturally looks to see if the use of them will contribute to his physical pleasure as well as his convenience, that the back of a chair is the right height and curvature to fit his back, and the seat is not so deep as to strain his legs; that the table or desk is one he can spread his legs under in natural fashion, and rest his elbows upon with ease; in short, that the furniture conforms to his bodily requirements, as the chair and bed of the "wee teeny bear" suited exactly the little old woman of Southey's tale. Last of all, the aesthetic pleasure, the appreciation of beauty by the mind, decides the choice in cases of equal unity and comfort. The artistic considerations are so many that furniture has become a branch of art, like sculpture or painting, with a large literature and history of its own.

Since most authorities on the subject largely ignore the question of utility and comfort, devoting themselves to the questions of aesthetic style, it will be useful to our purpose here to confine the discussion to the neglected qualities. As a rule, a durable, useful, and comfortable article is a beautiful one. At least it has the beauty of "grace," by which terms the old writers on aesthetics characterized perfect adaptation to purpose, and the beauty of what they called "homeliness," or, as we would now say,

since this term has been perverted, of "hominess," the suggestion of adding to the pleasure
of the household.

The quality of "hominess" is greatly increased
in an article of furniture by a frank look or
"home-made" appearance. There is no more
delightful occupation for the leisure hours of
man or woman, and no more useful training
for a boy or girl, than the making of simple
articles of home furniture. Really, the first article of furniture which should be brought into
the house is a well-equipped tool-chest, and the
first room which should be fitted up is the
workshop. A vast amount of labor will be saved
thereby in unpacking, adjusting, repairing and
polishing the old and the new household articles, so that life in the new home be begun
under the favorable auspices of the great household deity, the Goddess of Order. When it is
further considered that often small repairs made
by a carpenter cost more than a new article, the
tool-chest will be valued by the family as a most
profitable investment.

If it is not possible to procure the proper
materials and tools for making the entire article, some part of the work, the shaping, and
certainly the staining and polishing, can be

done at home. If the visitor does not recognize the home quality in such an article, the maker does, and will always have a pride and affection for it.

Many furniture manufacturer give in their catalogues designs of semi-made or "knock together" furniture, that is, the parts of tables, chairs, etc., cut out and planed, which it is intended that the purchaser put together himself. These, as a rule, are made of good material befitting the hand workmanship which will be put upon them, and are offered at a considerable reduction from the price asked for ready-made furniture of the same material.

Furniture stains of excellent quality are found in every hardware store and paint shop, which can easily be applied by the merest amateur.

It is never wise to buy flimsy furniture, however cheap. As a rule, there is too much furniture in the American home. It is better to get along with a few good, durable articles, even though a little expensive, than with a profusion of inferior ones. These soon reveal their "cheap and nasty qualities," are in constant need of repair, and quickly descend from the place of honor in the parlor to be endured a while in the living room, then abused in the kitchen, and, finally, burnt as fuel. Good wood and leather, however, are long in becoming shabby, and even then require only a little attention to be restored to good condition. When it is considered that in furniture there is virtually no monopoly of design or invention, and one therefore pays for material and labor alone, and competition has reduced these to the lowest terms, the purchaser is certain to get the worth of his money when he pays a higher price for durable material and honest workmanship. When it is further recalled that our chief heirlooms from the former generations are tables and chairs and bureaus, it will appear that it is our duty to hand down to our children furniture of similar durability and honest quality. Therefore, money spent for good furniture may be considered as a permanent investment whose returns are comfort and satisfaction in the present, and loving remembrance in the days to come.

So often is the artistic beauty of a house destroyed by a bad selection and arrangement of furniture and choice of inharmonious decorations, that many architects are coming to advise, and even dictate, the style of everything that goes into the house. Thus Colonial furniture is prescribed for a residence in Colonial style, Mission furniture for Mission architecture, etc. There is a corresponding movement among makers of artistic furniture to plan houses suited to their particular styles. Thus "Craftsman" houses and "Craftsman" furniture are designed by the same business interest.

Since, however, the average American home is something of a composite in architectural design, the housekeeper may be permitted to exercise her taste in making selections from the infinite variety of styles of furniture that are offered her by the manufacturers of the country. It is advisable, however, that the furniture in each room be in harmony.

Let us briefly examine the articles of furniture and styles of decoration appropriate for the several rooms.

The hall, now often the smallest, most ill-considered part of the house, was once its chief glory. In the old days in England, and, indeed, in America, the word was used as synonymous with the mansion, as Bracebridge Hall, Haddon Hall, etc. It was the largest apartment, the center of family and social life. Here the inmates and their guests feasted and danced and sang. Gradually it was divided off into rooms for specific purposes, until now in general practice it has narrowed down to a mere vestibule or entrance to the other rooms, with only those articles of furniture in it which are useful to the one coming in or going out of the house, combination stands with mirror, pins for hanging up hats and overcoats, umbrella holder, a chair or so, or a settee for the guest awaiting reception, etc. Often the chair or settee is of the most uncomfortable design, conspiring with the narrow quarters to make the visitor's impression of the house and its inmates a very disagreeable one. If space is lacking to make the hall a comfortable and pleasing room, it should be abolished, and the visitor, if a social one, taken at once to the parlor, and if a business one, to the living-room.

Where, however, size permits it, the hall should be made the most attractive part of the house. Here is the proper place for a "Grandfather's Clock," a rug or so of artistic design, and a jardinière holding growing plants or flowers. The wallpaper should be simple and dignified in design, but of cheerful tone. Some shade of red is always appropriate. Remember in choosing decorations that the colors of the spectrum—violet, indigo, blue, green, yellow, orange, red—run the gamut of emotive influence from depression to exhilaration. Violet and indigo lower the spirits, blue and green hold them in peaceful equilibrium, yellow begins to cheer them, and orange and red excite them.

However, the color scheme of a hall is largely dependent upon the wood-finish, because of the amount of this shown in the stairs.

Dark red is a very suitable color for the stair-carpet. The best way to fasten this is by a recent invisible contrivance which goes underneath the material. Brass rods are ornamental, rather too much so, and carpet tacks are provoking, both in putting down and taking up the carpet.

Where the hall and stairway are wide and room-like, pictures should be hung on the walls, interesting in subject and cheerful in decorative tone. The presence of the stairway, especially if this is broken by a landing, permits quite a variety of arrangement. The line of ascent should be followed only approximately. Remember that it is a fundamental law of art always to suggest a set idea, but never to follow it; to have a rule in mind, and then play about it rather than strictly pursue it. Art is free and frolicking. It gambols along the straight path of utility, following the scent of airy suggestions into outlying fields and by-paths, but always keeping the general direction of the path.

The parlor, when this is not combined with the hall, should be furnished and decorated according to the chief use the family intend to make of it. If they are given to formal entertainment, the color scheme may be in "high key," that is, a combination of white with either gold, rose, or green, any of which forms a bright setting for gay evening costumes. But this decoration is not advisable in the case of the average American home, since it is too fine and frivolous for the reception of neighbors in ordinary dress. A quieter, more dignified color-scheme should be adopted; such as golden brown, with subdued decorations for the wall, and écru-colored lace curtains for the windows. The floor may be of hardwood, in which case a few medium-sized Oriental rugs should be placed on the floor. It is not essential that these "match" the wallpaper for they are of the nature of artistic household treasures, and so rise autocratically above the necessity of conformity. Where they are chosen with a view to the color scheme, it is advisable to make them the means of transition from the hall. If this is decorated in dark red, the rugs leading from it into the parlor may shade off from this into more golden tones. The design of the rugs should be unobtrusive.

The homemaker should not feel that Oriental rugs are too expensive for consideration. Every once in a while there is a glut of them in the market, owing to an extensive importation, when they can be purchased at a price which will always insure the owner getting his money back if at any time he wishes to dispose of them. But the purchaser should be certain that the bargains offered are real ones, for rug-stores, like trunk-stores, always seem to be selling out "at a sacrifice." All Oriental rugs are well made, and, with proper usage, will last for generations, even enhancing in value. Therefore, they are always safe investments. Oriental rug-dealers repair rugs at a fair price for the time spent in doing so.

Since the floor space of a room with rugs in it is about two-thirds bare, the rugs will often not exceed the cost of a good carpet.

Hard woods take best a finish in brown or green, that gives an impress of natural texture impossible to secure by paint. Hardwood floors should be polished at least once a week with floor-wax, a simple compound of beeswax and turpentine, which can be made at home, or bought at the stores. This is useful for polishing any floor or woodwork. When the floor is not of hardwood, it may be stained. All varieties of stains are sold, the most durable, though the most expensive being the old-fashioned oil oak-stain. For the parlor and other floors, and corridors, stairways, etc., that do not get much wear, as well as for hardwood work in general, varnishing saves time and labor in cleaning.

For proper staining, the wood should be thoroughly scrubbed with soap and water; then, when dry, brushed over with hot size. Use concentrated size, a dry powder, rather than that in jelly form, as it is more convenient. It is dissolved and should be applied with a broad paint-brush. The application should be very rapid to prevent congealing and setting in lumps on the boards; accordingly the bowl containing the size should be set in boiling water until it is thoroughly liquid, and kept in this condition. The number of coats must depend upon the absorbent nature of the boards. One coat must be allowed to dry thoroughly before another is applied. Over night is a sufficient time for this. Varnishing also should be done rapidly to prevent dust settling on it. It is best done in a warm room, without draughts. Do not use stains ready-mixed with varnish, as these do not last as long, nor look so well as pure stains varnished after application. When the boards are in bad condition they should be first sandpapered. Cracks should be filled with wedges of wood hammered in and planed smooth. They can also be filled with thin paper torn up, mixed with hot starch and beaten to a pulp. This can be pressed into the cracks with a glazier's knife. The use of putty or plaster of Paris for this purpose is not so satisfactory as these methods.

For sleeping-rooms and living-rooms, which for sanitary reasons it is advisable to scrub, the stain should be left unvarnished.

CHAPTER VII

FURNITURE AND DECORATION

Housekeepers often prefer carpets to bare floors, and rugs for the reason that they "show the dirt" less. It is for this very reason that bare floors are best. Dirt is something to remove rather than conceal, and bare floors and rugs are more easily cleaned than carpets.

Covering the entire floor with plain filling, as a base for rugs, is an alternative for either hardwood or stained floors. It should be in the deeper tone of the color employed as a main part of the room's decoration.

When carpets are used, those in the hall, parlor, and dining-room should not be fitted into the corners, but a space should intervene between their edges and the walls. This may be filled with wood-carpetry, which, like all devices which suggest continuation of fine material through unseen parts, gives an air of art and elegance at comparatively little expense. Otherwise the floor, if hardwood, should be finished; if of other wood, stained and varnished. The carpet square is kept in position with brass-headed pins sold for the purpose.

Articles of furniture which are suitable for a parlor used chiefly as a reception room are light side chairs, and a settee, cane-seated with dark frames, or willow chairs, and settee, stained a dark hue, and brightened up with pretty cushions. These are not dear, so a little extra expense may be incurred in buying the parlor-table, which should be graceful in design and of rich dark wood, preferably mahogany, or in mahogany finish. A small table, of similar design and finish, should serve for afternoon tea, and a pretty desk stand near a window, with writing materials for the use of guests. There should be a clock upon the mantel-piece, ad a few other articles of vertu, such as a vase or so, a bronze statuette, etc., all harmonized by the common possession of artistic elegance.

The pictures in the parlor should possess evident artistic merit. There should be no suggestion of amateurishness. Family attempts at drawing or painting, crayon portraits, etc., all photographs, with the exception of those intended as artistic studies, should be excluded from the walls. If good originals by capable artists are not obtainable, fine engravings, etchings, and even colored copies of noted pictures may take their place.

A few books, well bound and with contents worthy of the binding, should lie on the parlor table, with a late magazine or so, for the entertainment of the waiting guest. There should be fresh flowers arranged in pretty bowls to add their impress of cheerfulness and beauty to the room.

In most American homes the parlor is also the music room. Since a piano should be chosen for quality rather than appearance, an instrument of any finish is allowable in a room, whatever its decorative scheme. Except in a family containing an expert performer, a piano should be chosen for softness and richness of tone, instead of brilliancy. For most households the old cottage organ is a more practicable instrument than the "concert grand" often found in a small parlor, where its piercing notes, especially in combination with operatic

singing, are so confined that tones and over-
tones, which should assist each other, mingle in
jarring confusion. Indeed, when the parlor is
large and high, a genuine pipe-organ built in a
recess and harmonizing in finish with the
woodwork of the room is not only the finest
decoration possible, but the most appropriate
musical instrument. Those families who possess
an old-fashioned piano, such as thin and tinkly
"square," are advised to have it overhauled and
refinished by a competent piano-repairer, and
preserved, if only for practice by the children.
In case such an instrument has "over-strung"
wires, it can be restored to a tone that is better
than that of the usual upright piano.

The parlor that is put to family use is usually
the best room to fit up for a library. In this case
the form-and-color scheme of furnishing and
decoration should differ entirely from that
when the room is used only for the reception
of guests. The furniture should be heavier and
larger, indicating utility, and its finish, as also
that of the walls, floor and woodwork, in deep
shades of the more restful colors of the spectrum. Sage-green is a good color for the
parlor-library. The furniture may be of this
or even darker hue. There is no better style of

furniture for the library than the Mission, made
comfortable by leather cushions. If leather is
thought too expensive, there are fair substitutes
for it in such materials as pantasote. But leather
should be procured if possible. It looks better
and wears longer, and even when shabby keeps
its respectability. With the Mission furniture
may be mingled an old-fashioned upholstered
chair or so, such as a large "Sleepy Hollow." A
Morris chair is almost as comfortable as this,
and perhaps upholds the dignity of the room a
little better, though it does not give the same
suggestion of "hominess." An old-fashioned
sofa, wide-seated, and designed to be laid upon,
should be placed in the room with its head
toward the light, so that the occupant may
read while reclining upon it. In almost every
old house there is a horse-lair sofa, either put
away in the attic or even in use, which can
be reupholstered to fit the color-scheme of
the room.

Books naturally form the chief ornament of
the library. It is a mistake to give them an elab-
orate casing. The simplest form is the best; the
shelves should run up evenly from the floor to
a more or less ornamental and somewhat projecting top, terminating several feet from the

ceiling. On this top a bust or so of an author may be appropriately placed, or copies of an ancient statue, and on the wall above, between the cases of shelves, may hang a few pictures, not necessarily bookish in suggestion, but reposeful in subject and tone, such as landscapes and marines.

A writing desk of comfortable size, with its chair, is essential in every library. It should be as far away as possible from the type of the modern business desk, and therefore an old-fashioned article with a sloping top, which, when let down, serves for the writing board, is an ideal form. Manufacturers continue to make these desks for home purposes.

The library table should be large and simple. One that is oval in shape is the best for the family to gather about, and therefore gives the most homelike appearance. The illumination of the library should center either upon this table, if a lamp is used, or above it, if gas or electric light. The desk should have a side-light of its own.

Modern library conveniences are presented in so handy and presentable shapes that the room may be perfectly equipped as a literary workshop without crowding it, or detracting from its appearance. A dictionary holder (wooden, not wire), a revolving bookcase for other works of reference, and a card index of the library may complete the equipment. It will be well to utilize one or more of the drawers of the desk as a file for clippings. These should be kept in stout manila envelopes, slightly less in size than the width and height of the drawer, and with the names of subjects contained, and arranged in alphabetical order.

The carpet should be plain in design, and underlaid with padding. The curtains should be of heavier and darker stuff than those in the parlor, and easily adjusted to admit the light.

The library and living room are generally next to each other, and so each may and should have a fireplace in the common chimney. That of the library should be of severer design; that of the living-room more homelike. Dutch tiles, with pictures that interest children, are specially appropriate for the latter.

Where the father of the family demands a "den" for reading and smoking, this may be a small room on the same general order as the library, but with an emphasis on comfort. Thus, the sofa should be replaced by a wide divan, which may also serve on occasion as a sleeping-place. The Turkish style of furnishing is the customary one; the Japanese style being a fad that came in with the aesthetic craze, was carried to an uncomfortable excess, and has gone out of fashion. The most appropriate style for an American house is American Indian. The brilliant and strikingly designed Navajo blankets may be used for both rugs and couch covers, or hung up as wall-ornaments. Moqui basketware serves equally well for useful purposes, such as scrap-baskets, and for ornamentation. The pottery of the Pueblo Indians, being naïve and primitive in design, is much more intimate and therefore appropriate than the Japanese bric-a-brac which it replaces.

The living-room is the heart of the house, and everything in it should be of a nature to collect loving associations. Almost any style of furniture is admissible into it, if only it is comfortable. There should be rocking-chairs, for the woman and the neighbors who drop in to see her, other chairs stout enough for a man to tip back upon the hind legs, and little chairs, or a little settee by the fireplace, for the children. The mother's desk should stand here, plainer than the one in the library, but of design similar to it; there should be a sofa as comfortable as the library one, to which the mother should have the first right. The paper should be cheerful in its tone with a definite design. This will become endeared by association with home to the children, and the mother should be slow to replace it. The window draperies may be home-made, such as of rough-finished silk or embroidered canvas, and the floor covered with a thick rag-carpet, preferably of a nondescript or "hit-and-miss" design. If the housekeeper thinks that this is "hominess" carried to excess, she may cover the floor with an ingrain carpet, or better, plain filling of a medium shade, on which a few rag rugs are laid, light in color. Very artistic carpets and rugs are made out of old carpets and sold at reasonable figures, and there still remain in some small towns throughout the country weavers who weave into carpets the carpet-rags sew together by housewives for the price of their labor alone.

There is a reason additional to its economy why this practice should not die out. The tearing up into strips of old garments, and the tacking of their ends together with needle and thread is work eminently suited for children, and one in which they take great pride, as it gives them a share in the creation of a useful an beautiful household article.

The dining-room should be decorated in accordance with the quantity of daylight it receives. It should be, if possible, a light room, with preferably the morning sun. In this case, it is properly furnished and decorated in dark tones, on the order of the library; if the room is dark, the furniture, wood-finish, and wall-paper should be warm and light in feeling. The housekeeper has a wide variety of sets of dining table and chairs to choose from. Whatever she selects should be distinguished by the quality of dignity. Here is the one room in the house where formality is thoroughly in place; it is at table where bad manners are wont most to show themselves among children, and laxity in etiquette among their parents. Just as the exclusive use of the room for eating purposes saves labor in housework, so will its dignity in decoration aid in enforcing the mother's teaching of good habits to the children.

Here, if anywhere in the house, plain wall-paper should be used, since the chief decorations are the china closet, cabinet and sideboard.

The dining-room ought not to have a fire-place or stove if other means of heating it are available, since heat, like food, should be equally distributed to those at table. Preference in seat-ing should be a matter of honor rather than of material advantage.

Comfort and cleanliness are the qualities which condition the equipment and decoration of the bed-room. When one considers that a third of a man's life is spent in bed, it will be seen how exceedingly important is the selection of this article of furniture. The essential parts of a good bed are spring and mattress, and no expense should be spared here in securing the best. The frame, which though the ornamental part is the least essential, is a matter of indifferent consideration. There is no better kind of bedstead than an iron or brass one, because of cleanliness and strength and the ease with which it may be taken apart and put together again. The pillows deserve almost equal consideration with the mattress. Since the feathers used in stuffing pillows may be cleaned, it is economical to see that these are of the best quality. Bed clothing is often selected under the mistaken impression that weight is synonymous with warmth, and heavy quilted comforts are chosen instead of lighter, woolen blankets. The pure woolen blanket is the ideal bed-covering and in various degrees of thickness may serve for all of the bed clothes save the sheets, and the light white coverlet, which is placed over all merely for appearance.

With increasing attention paid to hygiene, single beds rather than double are coming into favor. Even where two people occupy the same room they will be more comfortable in different beds. It is a mistake for young people and infants to sleep with older people, or for those who are well and strong with sickly or delicate persons, as there is apt to be a loss of vitality to the more vigorous party.

Everything connected with the bed should be regularly and thoroughly sunned and aired. The occupant on rising should throw back the bed-clothes over the foot of the bed, or, indeed, take them off and hang them over a chair in the sunlight.

The first thing in making a bed should be to turn the mattress. The lower sheet is then put on right side up and with the large end at the top. This is tucked in carefully all around, then the covering sheet is put on with the large end at the top, but the right side under. This is tucked in only at the foot in order to permit the bed to be easily entered. Over these the blankets are placed and folded back at the head under the fold of the upper sheet. Pillow-shams should never be used, as ornamentation on a bed is not necessary, and if it were a sham is never an ornament.

The walls of bedrooms may very properly be painted, as also the floors, to permit scrubbing, especially after the illness of an occupant. If papered, a chintz pattern is preferable; cretonne of similar design should then be used for furniture slips, etc. The woodwork may be white, with the chairs to match. There should be washable cotton rag-rugs, loosely woven to be grateful to the bare feet, at the bedside and in front of the bureau, dressing-table and doorway. Where space is limited, a combined bureau and dressing-table, or even a chiffonier with a mirror, may be used.

A child's bedroom may very appropriately have a wall-paper of a design intended to interest it, such as representations of animals, scenes from Mother Goose, etc. This is also suitable for the nursery.

The guest-room has come to be the *chamber de luxe* of the house, the place in which every conceivable article is introduced that might be required by the visitor, all being of expensive quality. Probably it is best to conform to this practice, since it is an expected thing, but money spent on the guest-room beyond that necessary to make it simply the best bedroom in the house, brings smaller returns in usage than anywhere else. The average guest is more pleased with a room such as he sleeps in himself at home than with one where elegance seems too fine for the use. It was a plainsman, who, being lodged in such a room on a visit to civilization, slept on the floor rather than touch the immaculate pillow-shams and bed-cover, which he conceived to be parts of the bed clothing not designed for use.

The window-shades of a house, since they show without, should be uniform in color, and no attempt be made to suit the individual decoration of a room to them. The material should be plain Holland, white or buff when there are outside blinds, otherwise green or blue. In recent years shutters, or outside blinds, have come somewhat into disuse. This is, on the whole, perhaps an improvement, for they are rarely manipulated with judgment, being either left open or kept shut for continuous periods. In the latter case they darken rooms which, though unused, would have been better for the admission of sunlight. The reason for this lack of manipulation is that they are opened and fastened with difficulty from the inside. All the purpose of the outside blinds is served by inside blinds, which are much more easily operated, and lend themselves admirably to decoration. One form of these, known as Venetian blinds, consisting of parallel wooden slats, strung on tapes, is coming again into vogue. They are cheaper than the usual sort of blinds, and are very durable as well as artistic. After all, however, shades are the most practical form of modulating the entrance of light into a house.

CHAPTER VIII

THE MOTHER

Nursing the Child—The Mother's Diet—Weaning—The Nursing-bottle—Milk for the Baby—Graduated Approach to Solid Diet—The Baby's Table Manners—His Bath—Cleansing His Eyes and Nose—Relief of Colic—Care of the Diaper.

> But one upon earth is more beautiful and better than the wife—that is the mother.
> L. SCHEFER.

Tennyson says, "The bearing and the training of a child is woman's wisdom." Herein nature is ever urging her to the proper course. Thus the love of the newborn infant prompts the mother to feed him with her own milk, and this supplies exactly the elements he requires for healthy development. No other milk, however skillfully modulated, no "infant's food," however scientifically prepared, can fully take its place.

Unless illness prevents her from feeding her own child, or she is of a moody and unhappy disposition, it is the mother's place to give her breast to the infant. The condition of mind of the mother has a great deal to do with the quality of the milk. A despondent and excitable temperament is often more productive of harm than a low physical condition. It is hardly necessary to warn the mother to be careful of her diet, as this has immediate effect on the quality of the milk. Of course, any drink containing alcohol must be avoided. Tea and coffee, expect when taken in weak strength, have also a deleterious effect. Milk, and next to it, cocoa, are the best beverages for the mother. Mothers should also avoid taking medicine except when positively required.

There is no need for the mother to vary greatly her solid diet. She will naturally select that which is most nutritious and easily digested. Anything that tends to make her costive, such as fruits or green vegetables, should be partaken of with discrimination.

The baby should be fed with systematic regularity from the beginning. While a child does not need food for the first day after birth, nevertheless it is well to put it to the breast about six hours after birth, since for the first few days after child-birth the breasts secrete a laxative element which acts as a sort of physic upon the child, clearing its bowels of a black, tarry substance, that fills them. The full supply of normal milk comes after the third day. After the first feeding the baby should be put to the breast every four hours for the first day and after that every two hours, being kept there about twenty minutes each time. The mother should be watchful and see that the child is awake and is nursing. Even at this early age it can be compelled to learn a good habit. Unless it learns this habit, the mother will be put to great inconvenience and the baby will suffer because of the disarrangement of the systematic feeding. If he is allowed to nurse at his own pleasure, the results will quickly make themselves manifest in the form of colic, leading to wakefulness and bad temper.

A baby should not remain awake more than four hours in the day on the whole, and he should be so trained that the eight hours from ten o'clock at night to six in the morning, when his mother is sleeping, should be for him also an uninterrupted period of slumber.

The baby should be weaned at ten months unless he is unwell at the time or the weaning comes in the heat of the summer, when there is danger of his becoming sickly or peevish.

Preparatory to weaning, the baby should be accustomed to the bottle. Provided the bottle holds half a pint or four glasses, the number of bottles may be increased from one a day at four months to two or six at eight months. The baby should certainly be weaned by the time it is a year old, as, even though the mother continues to have a plentiful supply of milk, this is not suited to his needs at this stage of his physical development. By this method of approach the act of permanently refusing the breast to the child will not greatly offend him. After a little crying he will philosophically accept the situation and reconcile himself the substitute.

Weaning is rendered easier by selecting a nursing-bottle which has the nipple in the shape of the breast. Care should be taken that the hole in the nipple is not too large, supplying more milk than the stomach can take care of as it comes, and so causing stomachic disorder. The nursing bottle should at all times be kept thoroughly clean by rinsing in hot water and washing in hot soapsuds. The milk for the child's bottle should, wherever possible, be what is called "certified," that is, the milk from a herd of cows which have been declared by the proper authorities to be all in good health, and which have been milked under sanitary conditions. This milk is delivered in clean, sealed bottles, preventing the admission of any dirt or deleterious substance from the time it leaves the dairy till opened. The milk for the baby should not be purchased from the can.

Milk that has been sterilized, that is, bottled and put in boiling water for an hour, is not so good for the baby as pasteurized milk; that is, milk kept at something less than the boiling point for half an hour, since the higher temperature causes the milk to lose some of the qualities beneficial to the child.

Since cow's milk differs in its constituents from mother's, having more fat and less sugar, there will be need at first to modify the cow's milk, weakening and sweetening it somewhat. One good recipe for modifying cows' milk is: One part milk, two parts cream, two parts lime-water, three parts sugar water, the sugar water being made by putting two even teaspoonfuls of sugar of milk in a pint of water.

Condensed milk, which is often used as a substitute for cows' milk, is not nearly so good, since it has lost in the process of condensation one of the most important elements, that which forms bone tissue. Accordingly, babies fed upon condensed milk are apt to be "rickety," and they lack in general power to resist disease, which is primarily the mark of a baby fed on mother's milk, and to a slightly lesser degree, one fed upon cows' milk.

The stomach grows very rapidly during infancy, increasing from a capacity of one ounce soon after birth to eight ounces at the end of the year, and this should be taken into account by the increase of the amount supplied it. After the first week, a baby should increase in weight at the rate of one pound a month for the first six months. If he falls behind this rate and remains healthy, more sugar and fat may be introduced into his milk. If, however, he fails to gain weight and is sickly, the milk should be diluted and modified so as to make it easier of digestion.

Every mother should be warned against a common practice of starting the flow of milk from the nipple of the bottle by putting it in her mouth. Gums and teeth are rarely perfectly clean, and so form the favorite lurking place for disease germs, which, though they may not produce disease in the stronger body of the adult, may do so and often do so in the more susceptible physique of the child.

Just as the child was trained to the bottle while it was still taking the mother's milk, so it should be taught gradually to eat solids while it is fed upon the bottle. After the child has been weaned at the tenth month, he can be fed occasionally on the broths or beef juice as a substitute for one of the milk feedings. The broth is more of a stimulant than a food, aiding digestion rather than supplying nourishment.

During the eleventh month, the yolk of a soft boiled egg, mixed with stale bread crumbs, may be added to the diet, together with a little orange juice or prune jelly. The latter will tend to keep his bowels free.

After twelve months, the child may be gradually accustomed to eat stale bread, biscuit or toast, broken in milk, thoroughly cooked oatmeal and similar cereals, baked potatoes moistened with broth, mashed potatoes moistened with gravy, and rice pudding. The pudding is made of two tablespoonfuls of clean rice, half a teaspoonful of salt, one-third of a cupful of sugar in five cups of milk. Bake in buttered pudding dish for two to three hours in slow oven, stirring frequently to prevent rice from settling.

At the age of two years and a half the child may be permitted to eat meat, preferably roast beef or mutton, cooked rare, or minced roast poultry.

Even though sugar is a very essential ingredient in the child's diet, it is very unwise to let it have this outside of its regular diet. Pure candy does not hurt the child by impairing its digestion so much as by interfering with its appetite for plain food. The child should never be allowed to form an inordinate appetite for anything, as this is certain to cause a corresponding deficiency elsewhere in his diet.

Even worse than the practice of giving candy to very young children is that of teaching them to drink tea and coffee. These are pure stimulants, supplying no tissue-building element, and taking the place of nutritious beverages that do, such as milk and cocoa.

After a child is old enough to be permitted to partake with discrimination of the general food of the table, he should be allowed to eat with the family. From the beginning he should be taught table manners, the use of knife and fork and napkin, and the subordination of his wishes to those of older people.

Next to feeding the baby properly, the most important duty of the mother is to see that it is kept clean. Even in its nursing days, after each feeding, she should rinse its mouth out by a weak boracic acid solution, since particles of milk may remain there which may become a source of infection. It is well for similar reason to wash her own breasts with the solution.

A baby should be bathed regularly at about the same time each day. During the first days of a child's life, he should be sponged in a warm room, with water at blood heat. In removing the garments, the mother should roll the infant gently from side to side, rather than lift him bodily. It is well to have a flannel cloth or apron ready to cover the child when it is being undressed. The baby's face should be washed in clear water, firmly and thoroughly with a damp cloth, and dried by patting with the towel. Then soap should be added to the water and the other parts of the baby's body washed in it; first, the head, ears and neck, then the arms, one uncovered at a time, then, with the mother's hand reaching under the cover, the back, during which process the baby is laid flat on the stomach, then the stomach, and last, the legs, one at a time, the baby being kept covered by the flannel as much as these operations permit.

The eyes of infants are prone to inflammation, and therefore require special attention in the way of cleansing. This can be done best by the use of the boracic solution upon a fresh pledget of cotton. Be careful not to use the same piece of cotton for both eyes, and to burn it after use. When the nose is stopped with mucous, a similar means can be used for cleansing it.

Every mother should study the individual nature and disposition of her child, in order to know what to do for it when it cries, for a cry may mean over-feeding as well as under-feeding, colic, or a wet diaper. Colic is often quickly relieved by turning the baby upon his stomach and rubbing his back, or by holding him in front of the fire, or wrapping him in a heated blanket. In drying the baby his comfort will be greatly increased by the use of talcum powder. Of course, soiled diapers should not be put on a child again until they are thoroughly washed. It will save the mother much trouble if absorbent cotton is placed within the diapers to receive the discharges from the bowels. These should be afterwards burned.

Too many clothes is bad for a young baby. If his stomach be well protected by a flannel band and he is kept from draughts, his other clothing may be very light, especially in summer.

CHAPTER IX

THE MOTHER

When the child reaches the school-age especial care should be taken of his diet. He should not be allowed to have meat at breakfast, except a little bacon with his eggs, one of which may be allowed a school-child when young, two men when older. Well-cooked cereals, such as oatmeal and cream of wheat, should form the staple article of diet, thought these may be varied by the ready-to-eat breakfast foods, such as corn-flakes. He should always have either sound fresh fruit, or stewed fruit, to eat with the cereal. His bread should always be toasted. Muffins are better for him than pancakes or waffles, which, however, should be allowed him occasionally as a treat.

As this kind of a breakfast largely consists of starchy foods, it should be eaten slowly, as starch requires thorough mastication. The practice of allowing children to lie late in bed, and then gulp their breakfast down in a minute or so, in order not to be late to school, is most pernicious.

The luncheon put up for school-children may consist chiefly of sandwiches, preferably several small ones of different kinds rather than one or two large ones. Biscuit sandwiches are generally more palatable to a child than plain bread ones. Besides those made of cold meat, there should be at least one cheese or one salad-and-nut sandwich, and one jelly sandwich. A hard-boiled egg, preferably one that has been cooked for some time in water kept under boiling point, will vary this diet. Of course fruit, such as an apple, an orange, or a banana, forms the best dessert. Occasionally cake, gingerbread, sweet biscuit, or a piece of milk chocolate may be put in the basket for a pleasant surprise.

The supper of the school-child while young should be a simple one, something on the order of the breakfast. In the early days children were fed at night on hasty pudding, or mush-and-milk, (cornmeal), which is an ideal food when thoroughly prepared, the meal being slowly sprinkled into the pot, which was stirred constantly all the while. The North Italians prepare cornmeal in this fashion; the mush, which they call "polenta," forms an accompaniment of meat stews, thus affording all the elements of a "perfect ration." American cooks should employ cornmeal far more than they do. Mush in particular has the advantage possessed by King Arthur's bag-pudding, what cannot be eaten at night may be served "next morning fried." While fried food is, as a rule, not good at breakfast for any save one who has hard manual labor or physical exercise to perform, an exception may be made of fried mush and fried eggs, because their base is so nutritious that the heated fat can do little to impair their digestibility, while it certainly whets the appetite before eating, and pleases the palate when the food is in the mouth. It should be borne in mind that those foods which require much mastication ought especially to be made palatable in order to be chewed thoroughly. Therefore, starchy materials ought to be prepared in appetizing ways; on the other hand, meats, which require less mastication, may dispense with high seasoning and rich sauces, especially as they have their own natural flavors.

The mother should closely follow the work of the child at school and aid this in every way at home. She should patiently answer his many questions, except when she is convinced that he is not really in search of information, but is asking them merely for the sake of asking. Wherever the child ought to be able to reason out the answer, the mother should assist him to do so by asking him guiding questions in turn. This is the method that Socrates, the greatest of teachers and philosophers, employed with his pupils, and, indeed, with his own children. It is as useful in inculcating moral lessons as in teaching facts. When one of the sons of Socrates, Lamprocles, came to him complaining that the mother, Xanthippe, treated him so hardly that he could not bear it, the philosopher, by kindly questions, led the boy to acknowledge his great debt to her for her care of him in infancy and in sickness, and, by showing the many things Xanthippe had to try her patience, persuaded him to bear with her and to give her that love which was her due.

Where manual training is taught in the schools, the mother should give every opportunity to her children to practice it at home.

Where it is not a part of the school course, parents should study to devise home substitutes for it, the mother teaching the girls sewing, embroidery, etc., and the father instructing the boys in carpentry and the like.

The desire to collect things, which seizes boys and girls at an early age, should be turned into useful channels by teachers and parents. Often this valuable instinct is largely wasted, as in the collecting of postage-stamps, the impulse which it gives to geographical and historical investigation being grossly perverted—for example a little island, that once issued a stamp which is now rare, looming larger in importance than a great country none of the stamps of which have any special value.

Every school, or, failing this, every home, should have a museum, not so much of curiosities as of typical specimens. These may be geological, botanical, faunal or archaeological; the rocks and soils and clays of the home country, the flowers of plants and sections of wood of trees; the skins of animals and birds (taxidermy is a fascinating employment for the young) eggs and nests (here the child should be taught to be a naturalist and not a vandal), and Indian arrow-heads and stone-axes.

In this connection it should be suggested that the most valuable collection of all is a herbarium of the flowers of literature, specimens of which may be found in the home library. That a child is not fond of reading is testimony that his parents no less than his teachers have failed in their duty.

Above all, the parents should see that their boys and girls have facilities for that physical culture which is necessary for health and proper development. Those exercises which are both recreative and useful are preferable. Gardening may be made a delight instead of a hardship, if the child is allowed to enjoy the fruits of his labor. Let him sell the vegetables he raises to the family, and, if there is an excess, to the neighbors, for pocket money. He will enjoy purchasing his own clothing even more than using the money solely for his pleasures.

Healthful sports should be encouraged, and games, such as chess, that develops the intellect. There are many card games, such as "Authors," that impart useful instruction in literature, history, natural science, business, etc. Playing these in the home is a good thing no less for parent than child. Many a mother has acquired a well-rounded culture after her marriage through her determination to "keep ahead of the children" in their studies and intellectual activities.

The child should be early accustomed to take cold baths, and then run about naked in a room under the impulse given by the tingling glow of reaction. If a play is made of the bath the habit will be formed for life, and in this way, one of the mother's chief struggles, to make the children clean themselves, will be abolished. It is natural for a child to get dirty, and therefore it should be made as habitual an impulse for them to get clean again.

Of all such habits, keeping the teeth clean is most important. Children's teeth are a chief source of anxiety to the mother even before they make their appearance.

Troubles in teething are generally due to innutritious and illy-digested food. Sometimes, however, when the food is all right, the teeth will still have difficulty in coming through the gums. Whenever the mother observes that her crying child refuses to bring its gums together on anything, she should examine them, and, if they are swollen, have them lanced.

The "milk-teeth," even though they are temporary, should be looked after carefully, as their decay will often spread to the coming permanent teeth. Besides, they should be preserved as long as possible, and in the best condition, to aid in mastication. Accordingly, young children should be taught regularly to rinse out their mouths and to use a tooth-brush and tooth-powder.

A child should run barefoot as much as conditions and climate permit. When it wears shoes, these should conform as much as possible to the shape of the foot. With such footwear, the active child may form for life the habit of a natural gait, especially if parents will point out the beauty and advantages of this, and praise the men and women of their acquaintance who possess it. It is about the time when a girl is learning *Virgil* in the High School that she is tempted by vanity and the desire to be "like the other girls" to put on French heels. Then it is that the teacher or mother should quote to her the line of the *Aeneid* about Venus:

"The true goddess is shown by her gait,"

and save her from an irreparable folly.

If mothers will remember that children are not dolls, and that mothers are not children to take pleasure in bedecking them, they will need no advice about dressing their little ones. There is only one rule for her to follow: She should consult the comfort and health of the child, and, as far as consistent with these, the convenience to herself. It may be "cute" to dress a child like a miniature man or woman, but it is cruel to the child. There is no reason for distinguishing sex by dress in young children. "Jumpers" form the best dress for either a little boy or little girl in which to play. Even when they are older and a skirt distinguishes the girl, bloomers or knickerbockers of the same material beneath, approach the ideal of dress for comfort, health and decency more nearly than white petticoat and drawers. Indeed, the skirt is best when it is a part of a blouse, which is also a suitable dress for a boy.

A child should never be tortured with a large or stiff hat. The heads of children come up to the middles of men and women, and such a hat will be crushed in a crowd, and its poor little wearer placed in mortal terror. Indeed, children should be allowed to go bareheaded as much as possible, and, when they wear hats, have these simple in shape and soft in material. The plain cap is the best head covering for a boy. The girl's may be a little more ornamental, especially

in color. The universal seizure by the sex upon
the boy's "Tam o'Shanter" as peculiarly suited
for a play and school-hat, is therefore right
and proper. For a more showy style, lingerie
hats are justified. But the most beautiful and
appropriate form of the "best hat" for a little
girl is one of uniform material, straw, cloth or
felt, with simple crown, and wide, and more or
less soft brim, ornamented by a ribbon alone.
The addition of a single flower may be permitted, though this is like the admission of the
camel's nose into the tent,—it may lead to the
entrance of the hump—the monstrosity of the
modern woman's bonnet, which of late years
has by terms imitated a flower garden, a vegetable garden, an orchard, and, finally, with the
Chanticler fad, a poultry-yard.

The knickerbocker and the short skirt are
aesthetic, that is eye-pleasing, because they
mark a natural division of the body at the knee.
There is an artistic justification, therefore, in
mothers keeping their sons out of "long pants"
as long as possible, and in fathers (for it is they
who are the chief objectors) in opposing their
daughters' desire to don the dust-sweeping
skirt that marks attainment to womanhood.
Here, however, it is proper that the wishes of

the younger generation triumph. It is a social instinct to conform to the custom of one's fellows, and the children have reached "the age of consent" in matters of fashion. Their fathers and mothers may lend their influence to abolish foolish customs, or to modify them in the direction of wisdom, but it is best that this be in their capacity as citizens, and not as parents.

CHAPTER X

CARE OF THE PERSON

The Mother's Duty Toward Herself—Her Dress—Etiquette and Good Manners—The Golden Rule—Pride in Personal Appearance—The Science of Beauty Culture—Manicuring as a Home Employment—Recipes for Toilet Preparations—Nail-biting—Fragile Nails—White Spots—Chapped Hands—Care of the Skin—Facial Massage—Recipes for Skin Lotions—Treatment of Facial Blemishes and Disorders—Care of the Hair—Diseases of the Scalp and hair—Gray Hair—Care of Eyebrows and Eyelashes.

> Certainly this is a duty, not a sin.
> "Cleanliness is indeed next to godliness."
> JOHN WESLEY—*On Dress.*

In all her multitudinous concerns the housekeeper should not forget her duties toward herself. Many a mother in looking out that her children are a credit to the family in dress and manners and care of their persons, gives up all thought of standing as an exemplar of these things among the ladies of the community.

This is a sacrifice of self that is not commendable, since it defeats its purpose. The mother should always be herself an illustration of the lessons she teaches, else they will not be seriously considered.

It is impossible here to give more than a few general suggestions as to the dress and millinery of the mother. She should have a variety of simple house-dresses, suited to her various duties, and these should be kept as neat as possible. Each should be made for its purpose, not converted to it from one of her fine dresses. Nothing gives an impression of slatternliness more than the wearing about the house of a frayed and soiled garment "that has seen better days."

The best dresses and hats of a woman, even who goes little "into society," should also be sufficient in number and varied in style to suit the changing seasons of the year, and the widely differing occasions for use which occur in every station of life. The purchase of several good articles of attire rather than one or two is economical in the end. There is not only the obvious mathematical reason that, if one dress wears a year, four dresses must be bought in four years, whether this is done simultaneously or successively, but there is the physical reason that a dress, like a person, that has regular periods of rest, becomes restored in quality. Accordingly, all dresses should be laid very carefully away when not in use, and the proper means taken to refresh them.

Unfortunately the arbitrary and senseless changes in fashion render this practice hard to follow. No woman likes to look out of style. However, by a little cleverness garments and hats may be adapted to the prevailing mode (although the arbiters of fashion, in the interests of manufacturers, try by violent changes of style to render this impracticable). These adaptations may not be in the height of fashion, but they will be in good form and taste. Indeed, it is never good taste to follow extremes of style. The well-known lines of Pope on the subject hold true in every age:

> "....in fashions the rule will hold,
>   Alike fantastic if too new or old;
> Be not the first by whom the new are tried,
>   Nor yet the last to lay the old aside."

Some of the best-dressed women in artistic in musical circles design their clothes wholly to suit their personal appearance, with such success that their independence of the prevailing mode of large or small hats or sleeves, striped or checked fabrics, etc., wins universal admiration.

Remember that a dress or a hat is never a "creation" in itself. The wearer must always be considered. Short, stout women should avoid horizontal stripes or lines of ornamentation that call attention to breadth, and should choose those perpendicular stripes and lines which tend to give an impression of height and slenderness. A hat lining may be used to put rosiness into a pale face, and a color may be selected for a dress which will neutralize too much redness in the skin. But these are matters of common knowledge to all women. The trouble is, that in their desire to be "in style," many women forget, or even deliberately ignore these fundamental principles of art in dress. Fondness for a particular color, as a color, causes many women to wear it, regardless of its relation to their complexion; and there have been women of mystical mind who, believing that each quality of soul had its correspondent in a particular hue, wore those colors which they thought were significant of their chief traits of character— with weird results, as you may imagine.

It is unnecessary, in this book of "practical

suggestions," to discuss in detail the question of etiquette, which may be defined as "the prevailing fashion in social intercourse." Styles in visiting cards change from year to year, and the social usages of one city differ from another. If it is required to know these, the latest special work on etiquette should be procured.

The general principles of good manners, however, which lie at the basis of etiquette, just as good morals form the foundation of law, although there are discrepancies in both cases, may appropriately be presented here, though briefly.

Good manners and good morals alike follow the Golden Rule: "Whatsoever ye would that others should do to you, do ye even so to them." Egoism and selfishness are the bane of both. True politeness consists of considering the pleasure of others as a thing in itself, without regard to your own advantage. If an attention is paid, a gift given, a service rendered, these should be done solely for the recipient's happiness, not with a view to his making a return in kind, possibly with interest. It is good manners to call on people who will be pleased to see you; not on those whom you wish to see, but to whom you and your affairs are of no concern.

A first visit to a newcomer in town is right and proper. A stranger is presumed to be desirous of making friends, but the first call ought to indicate whether or not he and you have that community of interest which is essential to friendship. If you are the newcomer, it is your duty to show your appreciation of the attention by returning first calls, but you should so act that your hosts will feel free to continue the acquaintance if it will be agreeable to them, or discontinue if it is not. Indeed, in every situation you should give the other party this choice. Friendship is one of the most valuable forms of social energy, and it should be carefully conserved. Yet more than any other form it is wasted, because of a false regard for social conventions. At how many calls are both parties bored! How many persons—women in particular, who have not the man's freedom in selecting associates—continue in the treadmill round of an uncongenial social circle! To escape from this may require the special exercise of will, and the incurring of criticism, but these out to be assumed. However, in most cases, a woman may gradually escape from the distasteful circle and form new and more congenial friends without remark.

After the brightening effects on mind and spirits of social intercourse comes the advantage of toning up the personal appearance. A decent self-respect in dress should always be flavored with a touch of pride, for this is an excellent preservative. To have a proper pride, there must be the incentive of the presence of other people whose admiration we may win. Pride in dress is naturally conjoined with the care of the person. There is an excellent term for this, which, though borrowed from the stable, carries with it only sweet and wholesome suggestions. It is "well-groomed." A well-groomed woman is not only a well-gowned woman, but one who, like a favorite mare, is always spick and span in her person, and happy in her quiet consciousness of it. And every woman, whether she possesses a maid or not, indeed, whether she has fine gowns or not, may win the admiration of all her associates by her "grooming."

CHAPTER XI

GENERAL PRINCIPLES
OF COOKING

The Prevalence of Good Recipes for All Save Meat Dishes—Increased Cost of Meat Makes These Desirable—No Need to Save Expense by Giving Up Meat—The "Government Cook Book"—Value of Meat as Food—Relative Values and Prices of the Cuts of Meat

> We may live without poetry, music and art;
> We may live without conscience,
>   and live without heart;
> We may live without friends;
>   we may live without books;
> But civilized man cannot live without cooks.
>   ("OWEN MEREDITH")—*Lucile.*

All the other duties of the housewife are subsidiary to the great subject of preparing food for the household. The care of the home, the care of health, etc., all either bear upon this work or require ability to perform it.

With decks cleared for action, therefore, we will proceed to discuss the fundamental principles of cookery, the application of which, in the form of specific recipes, will follow in a separate chapter.

In the limited space which can be here devoted to the subject, it will be assumed that the housewife is a cook, and can follow plain directions, and that she is familiar with the methods of preparing the ordinary meals that are universal throughout the country. It will also be taken for granted that she has one or more general cook books containing a wide variety of recipes for the making of bread in its various forms, cakes, pies, omelettes, salads, desserts, etc., and the discussion will be confined to meats, wherein, owing to advancing prices, new economical methods of preparation are coming into practice, based upon a scientific knowledge of food values.

Vegetarianism and fruitarianism are becoming adopted by many households, less as a matter of principle than as a recourse from what are considered the present prohibitive prices of meats. Now the proper way to solve a problem is not to evade it, but to face it and conquer it, and this is eminently true of the meat problem. Granted that the proportion of family income devoted to food cannot be increased, it is a fact that, by an intelligent study of the food value of the different kinds of meat, and of economic ways of preparing them, the expense of living may be maintained at the former rate, if not, indeed, materially lessened, with a great increase in both the nutritive value and the palatability of the family meals.

The "new nationalism" of America, which, after all, is only the turning to newer needs of the old nationalism that gave homesteads to the people and supplied them with improved methods of agriculture, is rightly taking the lead in the scientific education of the house-keeper in this household economy.

With special regard to the requirements of the people in these days of rising prices, espe-cially of meats, the United States Department of Agriculture has issued a booklet, prepared by C.F. Langworthy, Ph.D., and Caroline L. Hunt, A.B., experts in nutrition connected with the Department, which gives authoritative infor-mation about the cheaper cuts of meat and the preparation of inexpensive meat dishes. This had become generally known as "The Government Cook Book." By the permission of the Department we here present portions of the information it contains, together with those recipes which best illustrate the principles of meat cookery for the home table.

VALUE OF MEAT AS FOOD

Considering the fact that meat forms such an important part of the diet, and the further fact that the price of meat, as of other foods, has advanced in recent years, it is natural for housekeepers to seek more economical methods of preparing meat for the table, and to turn their thoughts toward the less expensive cuts and ask what economy is involved in their use, how they may be prepared, and whether the less expensive dishes are as nutritious and as thoroughly and easily digested as the costlier ones.

The value of meat as food depends chiefly on the presence of two classes of nutrients, (1) protein or nitrogenous compounds, and (2) fat. The mineral matter it contains, particularly the phosphorus compounds, is also of much importance, though it is small in quantity. Protein is essential for the construction and maintenance of the body, and both protein and fat yield energy for muscular power and for keeping up the temperature of the body. Fat is especially important as a source of energy. It is possibly to combine the fat and protein of animal foods so as to meet the requirements of the body with such materials only, and this is done in the Arctic regions, where vegetable food is lacking; but in general it is considered that diet is better and far more wholesome when, in addition to animal foods, such as meat, which is rich in proteins and fats, it contains vegetable foods, which are richest in sugar, starch, and other carbohydrates. Both animal and vegetable foods supply the mineral substances which are essential to body growth and development.

The difference between the various cuts of meat consists chiefly in amount of fat and consequently in the fuel value to the body. So far as the proteins are concerned, i.e., the substances which build and repair the important tissues of the body, very little difference is found.

This general uniformity in proportion of protein makes it easy for the housekeeper who does not wish to enter into the complexities of food values to make sure that her family is getting enough of this nutrient. From the investigations carried on in the Office of Experiment Stations the conclusion has been drawn that of the total amount of protein needed every day, which is usually estimated to be 100 grams or 3½ ounces, one-half or 50 grams is taken in the form of animal food, which of course includes milk, eggs, poultry, fish, etc., as well as meat. The remainder is taken in the form of bread and other cereal foods and beans and other vegetables. The portion of cooked meat which may be referred to as an ordinary "helping," 3 to 5 ounces (equivalent to $3\frac{1}{2}$ to $5\frac{1}{2}$ ounces of raw meat), may be considered to contain some 19 to 29 grams of protein, or approximately half of the amount which is ordinarily secured from animal food. An egg or a glass of milk contains about 8 grams more, so the housekeeper who gives each adult member of her family a helping of meat each day and eggs, milk, or cheese, together with the puddings or other dishes which contain eggs and milk, can feel sure that she is supplying sufficient protein, for the remainder necessary will be supplied by bread, cereals, and other vegetable food.

The nutrition investigations of the Office of Experiment Stations show also that there is practically no difference between the various cuts of meat or the meats from different animals with respect to either the thoroughness or the ease with which they are digested. Therefore, those who wish to use the cheaper cuts need not feel that in so doing their families are less well nourished than by the more expensive meats.

RELATIVE VALUES AND PRICES OF THE CUTS OF MEAT

The relative retail prices of the various cuts usually bear a direct relation to the favor with which they are regarded by the majority of persons, the juicy tender cuts of good flavor selling for the higher prices. When porterhouse steak sells for 25 cents a pound, it may be assumed that in town or village markets round steak would ordinarily sell for about 15 cents, and chuck ribs, one of the best cuts of the forequarter, for 10 cents. This makes it appear that the chuck ribs are less than half as expensive as porterhouse steak and two-thirds as expensive as the round. But apparent economy is not always real economy, and in this case the bones in the three cuts should be taken into account. Of the chuck ribs, more than one-half is bone or other materials usually classed under the head of "waste" or "refuse." Of the round, one-twelfth is waste, and of the porterhouse one-eighth. In buying the chuck, then, the housewife gets, at the prices assumed, less than one-half pound of food for 10 cents, making the net price of the edible portion 22 cents a pound; in buying round, she gets eleven-twelfths of a pound for 15 cents, making the net value about $16\frac{1}{2}$ cents; in buying porter-house, she gets seven-eighths of a pound for 25 cents, making the net value about $28\frac{1}{2}$ cents a pound. The relative prices, therefore, of the edible portions are 22, $16\frac{1}{2}$, and $28\frac{1}{2}$ cents; or to put it in a different way, a dollar at the prices assumed will buy $4\frac{1}{2}$ pounds of solid meat from the cut, know as chuck, 6 pounds of such meat from the round, and only $3\frac{1}{2}$ pounds of such meat from the porterhouse. To this should be added the fact that because of the way in which porterhouse is usually cooked no nutriment is obtained from the bone, while by the long slow process by which the cheaper cuts, except when they are broiled or fried, are prepared the gelatin, fat, and flavoring material of the bone are extracted. The bones of meats that are cooked in water, therefore, are in a sense not all refuse, for they contain some food which may be secured by proper cookery.

It is true, of course, that the bones of the steaks may be used for soup making, and that the nourishment may thus be utilized, but this must be done by a separate process from that of cooking the steak itself.

TEXTURE AND FLAVOR OF MEAT

Although meats vary greatly in the amount of fat which they contain and to a much less degree in their protein content, the chief difference to be noted between the cheaper and more expensive cuts is not so much in their nutritive value as in their texture and flavor. All muscle consists of tiny fibers which are tender in young animals and in those parts of older animals in which there has been little muscular strain. Under the backbone in the hind quarter is the place from which the tenderest meat comes. This is usually called the tenderloin. Sometimes in beef and also in pork it is taken out whole and sometimes it is left to be cut up with the rest of the loin. In old animals, and in those parts of the body where there has been much muscular action, the neck and the legs for example, the muscle fibers are tough and hard. But there is another point which is of even greater importance than this. The fibers of all muscle are bound together in bundles and in groups of bundles by a thin membrane which is known as connective tissue. This membrane, if heated in water or steam, is converted into gelatin. The process goes quickly if the meat is young and tender; more slowly if it is tough. Connective tissue is also soluble in acetic acid, that acid to which the sourness of vinegar is due. For this reason it is possible to make meat more tender by soaking it in vinegar or in vinegar and water, the proportions of the two depending on the strength of the vinegar. Sour beef or "sauer fleisch," as it is known to Germans, is a palatable dish of this sort. Since vinegar is a preservative this suggests a method by which a surplus of beef may be kept for several days and then converted into a palatable dish.

Flavor in meat depends mainly on certain nitrogenous substances which are called extractives because they can be dissolved out or "extracted" by soaking the meat in cold water. The quality of the extractives and the resulting flavor of the meat vary with the condition of the animal and in different parts of its body. They are usually considered better developed in older than in very young animals. Many persons suppose extractives or the flavor they cause are best in the most expensive cuts of meat; in reality, cuts on the side of beef are often of better flavor than tender cuts, but owing to the difficulty of mastication this fact is frequently not detected. The extractives have little or no nutritive value in themselves, but they are of great importance in causing the secretion of digestive juices at the proper time, in the right amount, and of the right chemical character. It is this quality which justifies the taking of soup at the beginning of a meal and the giving of broths, meat extracts, and similar preparations to invalids and weak persons. These foods have little nutritive material in themselves, but they are great aids to the digestion of other foods.

The amount of the extractives which will be brought out into the water when meat is boiled depends on the size of the pieces into which the meat is cut and on the length of time they are soaked in cold water before being heated. A good way to hinder the escape of the flavoring matter is to sear the surface of the meat quickly by heating it in fat, or the same end may be attained by plunging it into boiling water. Such solubility is taken advantage of in making beef tea at home and in the manufacture of meat extract, the extracted material being finally concentrated by evaporating the water.

GENERAL METHODS OF
COOKING MEAT

The advantages of variety in the methods of preparing and serving are to be considered even more seriously in the cooking of the cheaper cuts than in the cooking of the more expensive ones, and yet even in this connection it is a mistake to lose sight of the fat that, though there is a great variety of dishes, the processes involved are few in number.

An experienced teacher of cooking, a woman who has made very valuable contributions to the art of cookery by showing that most of the numerous processes outlined and elaborately described in the cook books can be classified under a very few heads, says that she tries "to reduce the cooking of meat to its lowest terms and teach only three ways of cooking. The first is the application of intense heat to keep in the juices. This is suitable only for portions of clear meat where the fibers are tender. By the second method the meats are put in cold water and cooked at a low temperature. This is suitable for bone, gristle, and the toughest portions of the meat which for this purpose should be divided into small bits. The third is a combination of these two processes and consists of searing and then stewing the meat. This is suitable for halfway cuts, i.e., those that are neither tender nor very tough." The many varieties of meat dishes are usually only a matter of flavor and garnish.

In other words, of the three processes the first is the short method; it aims to keep all the juices within the meat. The second is a very long method employed for the purpose of getting all or most of the juices out. The third is a combination of the two not so long as the second and yet requiring so much time that there is danger of the meat being rendered tasteless unless certain precautions are taken, such as searing in hot fat or plunging into boiling water.

There is a wide difference between exterior and interior cuts of meat with respect to tenderness induced by cooking. When beef flank is cooked by boiling for two hours, the toughness of the fibers greatly increases during the first half hour of the cooking period, and then diminished so that at the end of the cooking period the meat is found to be in about the same condition with respect to toughness or tenderness of the fibers as at the beginning. On the other hand, in case of the tenderloin, there is a decrease in toughness of the fibers throughout the cooking period which is particularly marked in the first few minutes of cooking, and at the end of the cooking period the meat fibers are only half as tough as before cooking.

CHAPTER XII

GENERAL PRINCIPALS OF COOKING

Texture and Flavor of Meat—General Methods of Cooking Meat—Economics in Use of Meat.

A good idea of the changes which take place while meat is being cooked can be obtained by examining a piece of flesh which has been "cooked to pieces," as the saying goes. In this the muscular fibers may be seen completely separated one from another, showing that the connective tissue has been destroyed. It is also evident that the fibers themselves are of different texture from those in the raw meat. In preparing meat for the table it is usual to stop short of the point of disintegration, but while the long process of cooking is going on the connective tissue is gradually softening and the fibers are gradually changing in texture. The former is the thing to be especially desired, but the latter is not. For this reason it is necessary to keep the temperature below the boiling point and as low as is consistent with thorough cooking, for cooks seem agreed, as the result of experience shows, that slow gentle cooking results in better texture than is the case when meat is boiled rapidly. This is the philosophy that lies back of the simmering process.

Losses of elements vary considerably with the method of cooking employed, being of course greatest where small pieces of meat are subjected to prolonged cooking. The chief loss in weight when meat is cooked is due to the driving off of water. When beef is cooked by pan broiling—that is, searing in a hot, greased pan, a common cooking process—no great loss of nutrition results, particularly if the fat and other substances adhering to the pan are utilized in the preparation of gravy. When beef is cooked by boiling, there is a loss of 3 to 20 per cent, of material present, though this is not an actual loss if the broth is utilized for soup or in some similar way. Even in the case of meat which is used for the preparation of beef tea or broth, the losses of nutritive material are apparently small though much of the flavoring matter has been removed. The amount of fat found in broth varies directly with the amount originally present in the meat; the fatter the meat the greater the quality of fat in the broth.

The loss of water in cooking varies inversely with the fatness of the meat; that is, the fatter the meat the smaller the shrinkage due to loss of water. In cooked meat the loss of various constituents is inversely proportional to the size of the cut. In other words, the smaller the piece of meat the greater the percentage of loss. Loss also appears to be dependent somewhat upon the length of time the cooking is continued. When pieces of meat weighing 1½ to 5 pounds are cooked in water somewhat under the boiling point there appears to be little difference in the amount of material found in broth whether the meat is placed in cold water or hot water at the beginning of the cooking period. When meat is roasted in the oven the amount of material removed is somewhat affected by the character of the roasting pan and similar factors, thus the total loss in weight is naturally greater in an open than a closed pan as the open pan offers more opportunity for the evaporation of water. Judging from the average results of a considerable number of test, it appears that a roast weighing 6 pounds raw should weigh 5 pounds after cooking, or in other words the loss is about one-sixth of the original weight. This means that if the raw meat costs 20 cents per pound the cooked would represent an increase of 4 cents a pound on the original cost; but this increase would, of course, be lessened if all the drippings and gravy are utilized.

ECONOMIES IN USE OF MEAT

The expense for meat in the home may be reduced in several ways, and each housekeeper can best judge which to use in her own case. From a careful consideration of the subject it appears that the various suggestions which have been made on the subject may be grouped under the following general heads: Economy in selection and purpose so as to take advantage of varying market conditions; purchasing meat in wholesale quantities for home use; serving smaller portions of meat than usual or using meat less frequently; careful attention to the use of meat, bone, fat, and small portions commonly trimmed off and thrown away and the utilization of left-over portions of cooked meat; and the use of the less expensive kinds.

The choice of cuts should correspond to the needs of the family and the preferences of its members. Careful consideration of market conditions is also useful, not only to make sure that the meat is handled and marketed in a sanitary way, but also to take advantage of any favorable change in price which may be due, for instance, to a large local supply of some particular kind or cut of meat. In towns where there is opportunity for choice, it may sometimes be found more satisfactory not to give all the family trade to one butcher; by going to various markets before buying the housekeeper is in a better position to hear of variations in prices and so be in a position to get the best values. Ordering by telephone or from the butcher's boy at the door may be less economical than going to market in person as the range of choice and prices is of course more obvious when the purchaser sees goods and has a chance to observe market conditions. Each housekeeper must decide for herself whether or not the greater convenience compensates for the smaller range of choice which such ordering from description entails. No matter what the cut, whether expensive or cheap, it can not be utilized to the best advantage unless it is well cooked. A cheap cut of meat, well cooked, is always preferable to a dear one spoiled in the preparation.

There is sometimes an advantage in using canned meat and meat products, and, if they are of good quality, such products are wholesome and palatable.

That economy is furthered by careful serving at table is obvious. If more meat is given at each serving than the person wishes or habitually eats the table waste is unduly increased. Economy in all such points is important and not beneath the dignity of the family.

In many American families meat is eaten two or three times a day; in such cases the simplest way of reducing the meat bill would very likely be to cut down the amount used, either by serving it less often or by using less at a time. Deficiency of protein need not be feared when one good meat dish a day is served, especially if such nitrogenous materials as eggs, milk, cheese, and beans are used instead. In localities where fish can be obtained fresh and cheap, it might well be more substituted for meat for the sake of variety as well as economy. Ingenious cooks have many ways of "extending the flavor" of meat, that is, of combining a small quantity with other materials to make a large dish, as in meat pies, stews, and similar dishes.

By buying in large quantities under certain conditions it may be possible to procure meat at better prices than those which ordinarily pre-

vail in the retail market. The whole side or
quarter of an animal can frequently be obtained
at noticeably less cost per pound than when it
is bought by cut, and can be used to advantage
when the housekeeper understands the art and
has proper storage facilities and a good-sized
family. When a hind quarter of mutton, for
example, comes from the market the flank (on
which the meat is thin and, as good housekeepers believe, likely to spoil more easily than some
other cuts) should be cooked immediately, or, if
preferred, it may be covered with a thin layer of
fat (rendered suet) which can be easily removed
when the time for cooking comes. The flank,
together with the rib bone, ordinarily makes a
gallon of good Scotch broth. The remainder of
the hind quarter may be used for roast or
chops. The whole pig carcass has always been
used by families living on the farms where the
animals are slaughtered, and in village homes;
town housekeepers not infrequently buy pigs
whole and "put down" the meat. An animal six
months old and weighing about one hundred
pounds would be suitable for this purpose. The
hams and thin pieces of belly meat may be
pickled and smoked. The thick pieces of belly
meat, packed in a two-gallon jar and covered

with salt or brine, will make a supply of fat pork to cook with beans and other vegetables. The tenderloin makes good roasts, the head and feet may go into head cheese or scrapple, and the trimming and other scraps of lean meat serve for a few pounds of home-made sausage. In some large families it is found profitable to "corn" a fore quarter of beef for spring and summer use. Formerly it was a common farm practice to dry beef, but now it seems to be more usual to purchase beef which has been dried in large establishments. The general use of refrigerators and ice chests in homes at the present time has had a great influence on the length of time meat may be kept and so upon the amount a housewife may buy at a time with advantage.

In the percentage of fat present in different kinds and cuts of meat, a greater difference exists than in the percentage of proteids. The lowest percentage of fat is 8.1 per cent. in the shank of beef; the highest is 32 per cent. in pork chops. The highest priced cuts, loin and ribs of beef, contain 20 to 25 per cent. If the fat of the meat is not eaten at the table, and is not utilized otherwise, a pecuniary loss results. If butter is the fat used in making crusts for meat pies, and in preparing the cheaper cuts, there is little economy involved; the fats from other meat should therefore be saved, as they may be used in place of butter in such cases, as well as in preparing many other foods. The fat from sausage or from the soup kettle, or from a pot roast, which is savory because it has been cooked with vegetables, is particularly acceptable. Sometimes savory vegetables, onion, or sweet herbs are added to fat when it is tried out to give it flavor.

Almost any meat bones can be used in soup making, and if the meat is not all removed from them the soup is better. But some bones, especially the rib bones, if they have a little meat left on them, can be grilled or roasted into very palatable dishes. The "sparerib" of southern cooks is made of the rib bones from a roast of pork, and makes a favorite dish when well browned. The braised ribs of beef often served in high-class restaurants are made from the bones cut from rib roasts. In this connection it may be noted that many of the dishes popular in good hotels are made of portions of meat such as are frequently thrown away in private houses, but which with proper cooking and seasoning make attractive dishes and give most acceptable variety to the menu. An old recipe for "broiled bones" directs that the bone (beef ribs or sirloin bones on which the meat is not left too thick in any part) be sprinkled with salt and pepper (Cayenne), and broiled over a clear fire until browned. Another example of the use of bones is boiled marrow bone. The bones are cut in convenient lengths, the ends covered with a little piece of dough over which a floured cloth is tied, and cooked in boiling water for two hours. After removing the cloth and dough, the bones are placed upright on toast and served. Prepared as above, the bones may also be baked in a deep dish. Marrow is sometimes removed from bones after cooking, seasoned, and served on toast.

Trimmings from meat may be utilized in various "made dishes," or they can always be put to good use in the soup kettle. It is surprising how many economies may be practiced in such ways and also in the table use of left-over portions of cooked meat if attention is given to the matter. Many of the following recipes involve the use of such left-overs. Others will suggest themselves or may be found in all the usual cookery books.

CHAPTER XIII

RECIPES FOR MEAT DISHES

Trying out Fat—Extending the Flavor of Meat—
Meat Stew—Meat Dumplings—Meat Pies and Sim-
ilar Dishes—Meat with Starchy Materials—Turkish
Pilaf—Stew from Cold Roast—Meat with Beans—
Haricot of Mutton—Meat Salads—Meat with
Eggs—Roast Beef with Yorkshire Pudding—Corned
Beef Hash with Poached Eggs—Stuffing—Mock
Duck—Veal or Beef Birds—Utilizing the Cheaper
Cuts of Meat.

> "To be a good cook means the knowledge
> of all fruits, herbs, balms and spices, and of
> all that is healing and sweet in fields and
> groves, savory in meats. It means carefulness,
> inventiveness, watchfulness, willingness, and
> readiness of appliance. It means the economy
> of your great grandmother and the science
> of modern chemistry; it means much tasting
> and no wasting; it means English thorough-
> ness, French art, and Arabian hospitality; it
> means, in fine, that you are to be perfectly
> and always ladies (loaf-givers), and are to see
> that everybody has something nice to eat."
>
> –JOHN RUSKIN

RECIPES

(In these directions a *level* spoonful or *level* cupful is called for.)

TRYING OUT FAT

A double boiler is the best utensil to use in trying out small portions of fat. There is no danger of burning the fat, and the odor is much less noticeable than if it is heated in a dish set directly over the fire.

Common household methods of extending the meat flavor through a considerable quality of material which would otherwise be lacking in distinctive taste are to serve the meat with dumplings, generally in the dish with it, to combine the meat with crusts, as in meat pies or meat roll, or to serve the meat on toast and biscuits. Borders of rice, hominy, or mashed potatoes are examples of the same principles applied in different ways. By serving some preparation of flour, rice, hominy, or other food rich in starch with the meat we get a dish which in itself approaches nearer to the balanced ration than meat alone and one in which the meat flavor is extended through a large amount of the material.

MEAT STEW

5 pounds of a cheaper cut of beef.

4 cups of potatoes cut into small pieces.

⅔ cup each of turnips and carrots
cut into ½-inch cubes.

½ onion, chopped.

¼ cup of flour.

Salt and pepper.

Cut the meat into small pieces, removing the fat; try out the fat and brown the meat in it. When well browned, cover with boiling water, boil for five minutes and then cook in a lower temperature until the meat is done. If tender, this will require about three hours on the stove or five hours in the fireless cooker. Add carrots, turnips, onions, pepper, and salt during the last hour of cooking, and the potatoes fifteen minutes before serving. Thicken with the flour diluted with cold water. Serve with dumplings (see below). If this dish is made in the fireless cooker, the mixture must be reheated when the vegetables are put in. Such a stew may also be made of mutton. If veal or pork is used the vegetables may be omitted or simply a little onion used. Sometimes for variety the browning of the meat is dispensed with. When white meat, such as chicken, veal, or fresh pork is used, the gravy is often made rich with cream or milk thickened with flour. The numerous minor additions which may be introduced give the great variety of such stews found in cookbooks.

MEAT DUMPLINGS

2 cups flour.
4 teaspoonfuls baking powder.
⅔ cup milk or a little more if needed.
½ teaspoonful salt.
2 teaspoonfuls butter.

Mix and sift the dry ingredients. Work in the butter with the tips of fingers, add milk gradually, roll out to a thickness of one-half inch, and cut with biscuit cutter. In some countries it is customary to season the dumplings themselves with herbs, etc., or to stuff them with bread crumbs fried in butter, instead of depending upon the gravy to season them.

A good way to cook dumplings is to put them in a buttered steamer over a kettle of hot water. They should cook from twelve to fifteen minutes. If it is necessary to cook them with the stew, enough liquid should be placed upon the meat and vegetables.

Sometimes the dough is baked and served as biscuits over which the stew is poured. If the stew is made with chicken or veal it is generally termed a fricassee.

MEAT PIES
AND SIMILAR DISHES

Meat pies represent another method of combining flour with meat. They are ordinarily baked in a fairly deep dish the sides of which may or may not be lined with dough. The cooked meat, cut into small pieces, is put into the dish, sometimes with small pieces of vegetables, a gravy is poured over the meat, the dish is covered with a layer of dough, and then baked. Most commonly the dough is like that used for soda or cream-of-tartar biscuit, but sometimes shortened pastry dough, such as is made for pies, is used. This is especially the case in the fancy individual dishes usually called patties. Occasionally the pie is covered with a potato crust in which case the meat is put directly into the dish without lining the latter. Stewed beef, veal, and chicken are probably most frequently used in pies, but any kind of meat may be used, or several kinds in combination. Pork pies are favorite dishes in many rural regions, especially at hog-killing time, and when well made are excellent.

If pies are made from raw meat and vegetables longer cooking is needed than otherwise, and in such case it is well to cover the dish with a plate, cook until the pie is nearly done, then remove the plate, add the crust, and return to the oven until the crust is lightly browned. Many cooks insist on piercing holes in the top crust of a meat pie directly it is taken from the oven.

MEAT AND TOMATO PIE

This dish presents an excellent way of using up small quantities of either cold beef or cold mutton. If fresh tomatoes are used, peel and slice them; if canned, drain off the liquid. Place a layer of tomato in a baking dish, then a layer of sliced meat, and over the two dredge flour, pepper, and salt; repeat until the dish is nearly full, then put in an extra layer of tomato and cover the whole with a layer of pastry or of bread or cracker crumbs. When the quantity is small, it may be "helped out" by boiled potatoes or other suitable vegetables. A few oysters or mushrooms improve the flavor, especially when beef is used. The pie will need to be baked from half an hour to an hour, according to its size and the heat of the oven.

MEAT WITH
STARCHY MATERIALS

Macaroni cooked with chopped ham, hash made of meat and potatoes or meat and rice, meat croquettes—made of meat and some starchy materials like bread crumbs, cracker dust, or rice—are other familiar examples of meat combined with starchy materials. Pilaf, a dish very common in the Orient and well known in the United Sates, is of this character and easily made. When there is soup or soup stock on hand it can be well used in the pilaf.

TURKISH PILAF

½ cup of rice.
¾ cup of tomatoes stewed and strained.
1 cup stock or broth.
3 tablespoonfuls of butter.

Cook the rice and tomatoes with the stock in a double boiler until the rice is tender, removing the cover after the rice is cooked if there is too much liquid. Add the butter and stir it in with a fork to prevent the rice from being broken. A little catsup or Chili sauce with water enough to make three-quarters of a cup may be substituted for the tomatoes. This may be served as a border with meat, or served separately in the place of a vegetable, or may make the main dish at a meal, as it is savory and reasonably nutritious.

STEW FROM COLD ROAST

This dish provides a good way of using up the remnants of a roast, either of beef or mutton. The meat should be freed from fat, gristle, and bones, cut into small pieces, slightly salted, and put into a kettle with water enough to nearly cover it. It should simmer until almost ready to break in pieces, when onions and raw potatoes, peeled and quartered, should be added. A little soup stock may also be added if available. Cook until the potatoes are done, then thicken the liquor or gravy with flour. The stew may be attractively served on slices of crisp toast.

MEAT WITH
BEANS

Dry beans are very rich in protein, the percentage being fully as large as that in meat. Dry beans and other similar legumes are usually cooked in water, which they absorb, and so are diluted before serving; on the other hand, meats by the ordinary methods of cooking are usually deprived of some of the water originally present—facts which are often overlooked in discussing the matter. Nevertheless, when beans are served with meat the dish is almost as rich in protein as if it consisted entirely of meat.

Pork and beans is such a well-known dish that recipes are not needed. Some cooks use a piece of corned mutton or a piece of corned beef in place of salt or corned pork or bacon or use butter or olive oil in preparing this dish.

In the Southern States, where cowpeas are a common crop, they are cooked in the same way as dried beans. Cowpeas baked with salt pork or bacon make an excellent dish resembling pork and beans, but of distinctive flavor. Cowpeas boiled with ham or with bacon are also well-known and palatable dishes.

HARICOT OF MUTTON

2 tablespoonfuls of chopped onions.
2 tablespoonfuls of butter or drippings.
2 cups of water, and salt and pepper.
1½ pounds of lean mutton or lamb cut into
   2-inch pieces.

Fry the onions in the butter, add the meat, and brown; cover with water and cook until the meat is tender. Serve with a border of Lima beans, seasoned with salt, pepper, butter, and a little chopped parsley. Fresh, canned, dried, or evaporated Lima beans may be used in making this dish.

MEAT SALADS

Whether meat salads are economical or not depends upon the way in which the materials are utilized. If in chicken salad, for example, only the white meat of chickens especially bought for the purpose and only the inside stems of expensive celery are used, it can hardly be cheaper than plain chicken. But, if portions of meat left over from a previous serving are mixed with celery grown at home they certainly make an economical dish and one very acceptable to most persons. Cold roast pork or tender veal—in fact, any white meat can be utilized in the same way. Apples cuts into cubes may be substituted for part of the celery; many cooks consider that with the apple the salad takes the dressing better than with the celery alone. Many also prefer to marinate (i.e., mix with a little oil and vinegar) the meat and celery or celery and apples before putting in the final dressing, which may be either mayonnaise or a good boiled dressing.

MEAT WITH EGGS

Occasionally eggs are combined with meat, making very nutritious dishes. Whether this is an economy or not of course depends on the comparative cost of eggs and meat.

In general, it may be said that eggs are cheaper food than meat when a dozen costs less than $1\frac{1}{2}$ pounds of meat, for a dozen eggs weigh about $1\frac{1}{2}$ pounds and the proportions of protein and fat which they contain are not far different from the proportions of these nutrients in the average cut of meat. When eggs are 30 cents a dozen they compare favorably with a round of beef at 20 cents a pound.

Such common dishes as ham and eggs, bacon or salt pork and eggs, and omelette with minced ham or other meat are familiar to all cooks.

ROAST BEEF
WITH YORKSHIRE PUDDING

The beef is roasted as usual and the pudding made as follows:

3 eggs.
1 pink milk.
1 cupful flour.
1 teaspoonful salt.

Beat the eggs until very light, then add the milk. Pour the mixture over the flour, add the salt, and beat well. Bake in hissing hot gem pans or in an ordinary baking pan for forty-five minutes, and baste with drippings from the beef. If gem pans are used they should be placed on a dripping pan to protect the floor of the oven from the fat. Many cooks prefer to bake Yorkshire pudding in the pan with the meat; in this case the roast should be placed on a rack and the pudding batter poured on the pan under it.

CORNED-BEEF HASH WITH
POACHED EGGS

A dish popular with many persons is corned-beef hash with poached eggs on top of the hash. A slice of toast is sometimes used under the hash. This suggests a way of utilizing the small amount of corned-beef hash which would otherwise be insufficient for a meal.

Housekeepers occasionally use up odd bits of

other meat in a similar way, chopping and sea-soning them and then warming and serving in individual baking cups with a poached or shirred egg on each.

STUFFING

Another popular way to extend the flavor of meat over a large amount of food is by the use of stuffing. As it is impossible to introduce much stuffing into some pieces of meat even if the meat is cut to make a pocket for it, it is often well to prepare more than can be put into the meat and to cook the remainder in the pan beside the meat. Some cooks cover the extra stuffing with buttered paper while it is cooking and baste it at intervals.

MOCK DUCK

Mock duck is made by placing on a round steak a stuffing of bread crumbs well seasoned with chopped onions, butter, chopped suet or drip-ping, salt, pepper, and a little sage if the flavor is relished. The steak is then rolled around the stuff-ing and tied with a string in several places. If the steak seems tough, the roll is steamed or stewed until tender before roasting in the oven until brown. Or it may be cooked in a casserole or other covered dish, in which case a cupful or more of water or soup-stock should be poured around the meat. Mock duck is excellent served with currant or other acid jelly.

VEAL OR BEEF BIRDS

A popular dish known as veal or beef birds or by a variety of special names is made by taking small pieces of meat, each just large enough for an individual serving, and preparing them in the same way as the mock duck is prepared.

Sometimes variety is introduced by seasoning the stuffing with chopped olives or tomato. Many cooks prepare their "birds" by browning in a little fat, then adding a little water, covering closely and simmering until tender.

UTILIZING THE CHEAPER CUTS OF MEAT

When the housekeeper attempts to reduce her meat bill by using the less expensive cuts, she commonly has two difficulties to contend with—toughness and lack of flavor. It has been shown how prolonged cooking softens the connective tissues of the meat. Pounding the meat and chopping it are also employed with tough cuts, as they help to break the muscle fibers. As for flavor, the natural flavor of meat even in the least desirable cuts may be developed by careful cooking, notably by browning the surface, and other flavors may be given by the addition of vegetables and seasoning with condiments of various kinds.

CHAPTER XIV

RECIPES
FOR MEAT DISHES

Prolonged Cooking at Low Heat—Stewed Shin of Beef—Boiled Beef with Horseradish Sauce—Stuffed Heart—Braised Beef, Pot Roast, and Beef a la Mode—Hungarian Goulash—Casserole Cookery—Meat Cooked with Vinegar—Sour Beef—Sour Beefsteak—Pounded Meat—Farmer Stew—Spanish Beefsteak—Chopped Meat—Savory Rolls—Developing Flavor of Meat—Retaining Natural Flavor—Round Steak on Biscuits—Flavor of Browned Meat or Fat—Salt Pork with Milk Gravy—"Salt-Fish Dinner"—Sauces—Mock Venison.

PROLONGED COOKING
AT LOW HEAT

Meat may be cooked in water in a number of ways without being allowed to reach the boiling point. With the ordinary kitchen range this is accomplished by cooking on the cooler part of the stove rather than on the hottest part, directly over the fire. Experience with a gas stove, particularly if it has a small burner known as a "simmerer," usually enables the cook to maintain temperatures which are high enough to sterilize the meat if it has become accidentally contaminated in any way and to make it tender without hardening the fibers. The double boiler would seem to be a neglected utensil for this purpose. Its contents can easily be kept up to a temperature of 200°F., and nothing will burn. Another method is by means of the fireless cooker. In this a high temperature can be maintained for a long time without the application of fresh heat. Still another method is by means of a closely covered baking dish. Earthenware dishes of this kind suitable for serving foods as well as for cooking are known as casseroles. For cooking purposes a baking dish covered with a plate or a bean jar covered with a saucer may be substituted. The Aladdin oven has long been popular for the purpose of preserving temperatures which are near the boiling point and yet do not reach it. It is a thoroughly insulated oven which may be heated either by a kerosene lamp or a gas jet.

In this connection directions are given for using some of the toughest and less promising pieces of meat.

STEWED SHIN OF BEEF

4 pounds of shin of beef.
1 medium-sized onion.
1 whole clove and a small bay leaf.
1 sprig of parsley.
1½ tablespoonfuls of flour.
1 small slice of carrot.
½ tablespoonful of salt.
½ teaspoonful of pepper.
2 quarts of boiling water.
1½ tablespoonfuls of butter
   or savory drippings.

Have the butcher cut the bone in several pieces.
Put all the ingredients but the flour and butter
into a stewpan and bring to a boil. Set the pan
where the liquid will just simmer for six hours, or
after boiling for five or ten minutes, put all into
the fireless cooker for eight or nine hours. With
the butter, flour, and one-half cupful of the clear
soup from which the fat has been removed, make
a brown sauce; to this add the meat and the marrow removed from the bone. Heat and serve. The
remainder of the liquid in which the meat has
been cooked may be used for soup.

BOILED BEEF WITH
HORSERADISH SAUCE

Plain boiled beef may also be served with horseradish sauce, and makes a palatable dish. A little
chopped parsley sprinkled over the meat when

served is considered an improvement by many persons. For the sake of variety the meat may be browned like pot roast before serving.

STUFFED HEART

Wash the heart thoroughly inside and out and stuff with the following mixture, and sew up the opening: One cup broken bread dipped in fat and browned in the oven, 1 chopped onion, and salt and pepper to taste.

Cover the heart with water and simmer until tender or boil ten minutes and set in the fireless cooker for six or eight hours. Remove from the water about one-half hour before serving. Dredge with flour, pepper, and salt, or sprinkle with crumbs and bake until brown.

BRAISED BEEF, POT ROAST, AND BEEF A LA MODE

The above names are given to dishes made from the less tender cuts of meat. They vary little either in composition or method of preparation. In all cases the meat is browned on the outside to increase the flavor and then cooked in a small amount of water in a closely covered kettle or other receptacle until tender. The flavor of the dish is secured by browning the meat and by the addition of the seasoning vegetables. Many recipes suggest that the vegetables be removed before serving and the liquid be thickened. As the vegetables are usually extremely well seasoned by means of the brown fat and the extracts of the meat, it seems unfortunate not to serve them.

Of course, the kind, quality, and shape of the meat all play their part in the matter. Extra time is needed for meats with a good deal of sinew and tough fibers, such as the tough steaks, shank cuts, etc.; and naturally a fillet of beef, or a steak from a prime cut, will take less time than a thick piece from the shin. Such dishes require more time and perhaps more skill in their preparation and may involve more expense for fuel than the more costly cuts, which like chops or tender steaks may be quickly cooked, but to the epicure, as well as to the average man, they are palatable when rightly prepared.

HUNGARIAN GOULASH

2 pounds top round of beef.
A little flour.
2 ounces salt pork.
2 cups tomatoes.
1 stalk celery.
1 onion.
2 bay leaves.
6 whole cloves.
6 peppercorns.
1 blade mace.

Cut the beef into 2-inch pieces and sprinkle with flour; fry the salt pork until light brown; add the beef and cook slowly for about thirty-five minutes, stirring occasionally. Cover with water and simmer about two hours; season with salt and pepper or paprika.

From the vegetables and spices a sauce is made as follows: Cook in sufficient water to cover for twenty minutes; then rub through a sieve, and add to some of the stock in which the meat was cooked. Thicken with flour, using 2 tablespoonfuls (moistened with cold water) to each cup of liquid, and season with salt and paprika.

Serve the meat on a platter with the sauce poured over it. Potatoes, carrots, and green peppers cooked until tender, and cut into small pieces or narrow strips, are usually sprinkled over the dish when served, and noodles may be arranged in a border upon the platter.

Goulash is a Hungarian dish which has come to be a favorite in the United States.

CASSEROLE COOKERY

A casserole is a heavy earthenware dish with a cover. A substitute for it can easily by improvised by using any heavy earthenware dish with a heavy plate for the cover. A casserole presentable enough in appearance to be put on the table serves the double purpose of baking and serving dish.

A suitable cut of beef or veal, and it may well be one of the cheaper cuts, as the long, slow cooking insures tenderness, may be cooked in a casserole.

Poultry and other meats besides beef or veal can be cooked in this manner. Chicken cooked in a casserole, which is a favorite and expensive dish in good hotels and restaurants, may be easily prepared in the home, and casserole cookery is to be recommended for tough chicken.

The heat must be moderate and the cooking must occupy a long time. Hurried cooking in a casserole is out of the question. If care is taken in this particular, and suitable seasonings are used, few who know anything of cooking should go astray.

Chopped meat also may be cooked in a casserole and this utensil is particularly useful for the purpose, because the food is served in the same dish in which it is cooked and may easily be kept hot, a point which is important with chopped meats, which usually cool rapidly.

MEAT COOKED WITH VINEGAR

Dishes of similar sort as regards cooking, but in which vinegar is used to give flavor as well as to soften the meat and make it tender, are the following:

SOUR BEEF

Take a piece of beef from the rump or the lower round, cover with vinegar or with a half-and-half mixture of vinegar and water, add sliced onion, bay leaves, and a few mixed whole spices and salt. Allow to stand a week in winter or three or four days in summer; turn once a day and keep covered. When ready to cook, brown the meat in fat, using an enameled iron pan, strain the liquid over it and cook until tender; thicken the gravy with flour or ginger snaps (which may be broken up first), strain it, and pour over the sliced meat. Some cooks add cream.

SOUR BEEFSTEAK

Round steak may be cooked in water in which there is a little vinegar, or if the time is sufficient, it may be soaked for a few hours in vinegar and water and then cooked in a casserole or some similar way.

POUNDED MEAT

Pounding meat before cooking is an old-fashioned method of making it tender, but while it has the advantage of breaking down the tough tissues it has the disadvantage of being likely to drive out the juices and with them the flavor. A very good way of escaping this difficulty is pounding flour into the meat; this catches and retains the juices. Below are given the recipes for two palatable dishes in which this is done:

FARMER STEW

Pound flour into both sides of a round steak, using as much as the meat will take up. This may be done with a meat pounder or with the edge of a heavy plate. Fry in drippings, butter, or other fat, in a Scotch bowl, or if more convenient in an ordinary iron kettle or a frying pan; then add water enough to cover it. Cove the dish very tightly so that the steam cannot escape and allow the meat to simmer for two hours or until it is tender. One advantage of this dish is that ordinarily it is ready to serve when the meat is done as the gravy is already thickened. However, if a large amount of fat is used in the frying, the gravy may not be thick enough and must be blended with flour.

SPANISH BEEFSTEAK

Take a piece of round steak weighing two pounds and about an inch thick; pound until thin, season with salt and Cayenne pepper, cover with a layer of bacon or salt pork, cut into thin slices, roll and tie with a cord. Pour around it half a cupful of milk and half a cupful of water. Place in a covered baking dish and cook two hours, basting occasionally.

CHOPPED MEAT

Chopped meat is one of the principal methods of making tough and inexpensive meat tender, i.e., dividing it finely and thus cutting the connective tissue into small bits. Such meats have another advantage in that they may be cooked quickly and economically.

Chopped raw meat of almost any kind can be very quickly made into a savory dish by cooking it with water or with water and milk for a short time, then thickening with butter and flour, and adding different seasonings as relished, either pepper and salt alone, or onion juice, celery, or tomato. Such a dish may be made to "go further" by serving it on toast or with a border of rice or in some similar combination.

SAVORY ROLLS

Savory rolls in great variety are made out of chopped meat either with or without egg. The variety is secured by the flavoring materials used and by the sauces with which the baked rolls are served. A few recipes will be given below. While these definite directions are given it should be remembered that a few general principles borne in mind make recipes unnecessary and make it possible to utilize whatever may happen to be on hand. Appetizing rolls are made with beef and pork mixed. The proportion varies from two parts of beef and one of pork to two of pork and one of beef. The rolls are always improved by laying thin slices of salt pork or bacon over them, which keep the surface moistened with fat during the roasting. These slices should be scored on the edge, so that they will not curl up in cooking. The necessity for the salt pork is greater when chopped meat is chiefly beef than when it is largely pork or veal. Bread crumbs or bread moistened in water can always be added, as it helps to make the dish go farther. When onions, green peppers, or other vegetables are used, they should always be thoroughly cooked in fat before being put in the roll, for usually they do not cook sufficiently in the length of time it takes to cook the meat. Sausage makes a good addition to the roll, but it is usually cheaper to use unseasoned pork meat with the addition of a little sage.

DEVELOPING FLAVOR OF MEAT

The typical meat flavors are very palatable to most persons, even when they are constantly tasted, and consequently the better cuts of meat in which they are well developed can be cooked and served without attention being paid especially to flavor. Careful cooking aids in developing the natural flavor of some of the cheaper cuts, and such a result is to be sought wherever it is possible. Browning also brings out flavors agreeable to most palates. Aside from these two ways of increasing the flavor of the meat itself there are countless ways of adding flavor to otherwise tasteless meats. The flavors may be added in preparing the meat for cooking, as in various seasoned dishes already described, or they may be supplied to cook meat in the form of sauces.

Retaining Natural Flavor

As has already been pointed out, it is extremely difficult to retain the flavor-giving extractives in a piece of meat so tough as to require prolonged cooking. It is sometimes partially accomplished by first searing the exterior of the meat and thus preventing the escape of the juices. Another device, illustrated by the following recipe, is to let them escape into the gravy which is served with the meat itself. A similar principle is applied when roasts are basted with their own juice.

ROUND STEAK ON BISCUITS

Cut round steak into pieces about one-half inch square, cover with water and cook it at a temperature just below the boiling point until it is tender, or boil for five minutes, and while still hot put into the fireless cooker and leave it for five hours. Thicken the gravy with flour mixed with water, allowing two level tablespoonfuls to a cup of water. Pour the meat and gravy over split baking-powder biscuits so baked that they have a large amount of crust.

FLAVOR OF BROWNED MEAT OR FAT

Next to the unchanged flavor of the meat itself comes the flavor which is secured by browning the meat with fat. The outside slices of roast meat have this browned flavor in marked degree. Except in the case of roasts, browning for flavor is usually accomplished by heating the meat in a frying pan in fat which has been tried out of pork or in suet or butter. Care should be taken that the fat is not scorched. The chief reason for the bad opinion in which fried food is held by many is that it almost always means eating burned fat. When fat is heated too high it splits up into fatty acids and glycerin, and from the glycerin is formed a substance (acrolein) which has a very irritating effect upon the mucous membrane. All will recall that the fumes of scorched fat make the eyes water. It is not surprising that such a substance, if taken into the stomach, should cause digestive disturbance. Fat in itself is a very valuable food, and the objection to fried foods because they may be fat seems illogical. If they supply burned fat there is a good reason for suspicion. Many housekeepers cook bacon in the oven on a wire broiler over a pan and believe it more wholesome than fried bacon. The reason, of course, is that thus cooked in the oven there is less chance for the bacon becoming impregnated with burned fat. Where fried salt pork is much used good cooks know that it must not be cooked over a very hot fire, even if they have never heard of the chemistry of burned fat. The recipe for bean-pot roast and other similar recipes may be varied by browning the meat or part of it before covering with water. This results in keeping some of the natural flavoring within the meat itself and allowing less to go into the gravy. The flavor of veal can be very greatly improved this way.

The following old-fashioned dishes made with pork owe their savoriness chiefly to the flavor of browned fat or meat:

SALT PORK WITH MILK GRAVY

Cut salt or cured pork into thin slices. If very salt, cover with hot water and allow it to stand for ten minutes. Score the rind of the slices and fry slowly until they are a golden brown. Make a milk gravy by heating flour in the fat that has been tried out, allowing two tablespoonfuls of fat and two tablespoonfuls of flour to each cup of milk. This is a good way to use skim milk, which is as rich in protein as whole milk. The pork and milk gravy served with boiled or baked potatoes makes a cheap and simple meal, but one that most people like very much. Bacon is often used in place of salt pork in making this dish.

"SALT-FISH DINNER"

½ pound salt pork.
1 pound codfish.
2 cups of milk (skim milk will do).
4 tablespoonfuls flour.
A speck of salt.

Cut the codfish into strips, soak in lukewarm water and then cook in water until tender, but do not allow the water to come to the boiling point except for a very short time as prolonged boiling may make it tough. Cut the pork into one-fourth inch slices and cut several gashes in each piece. Fry very slowly until golden brown, and remove, pouring off the fat. Out of four tablespoonfuls of the fat, the flour, and the milk make a white sauce. Dish up the codfish with pieces of pork around it and serve with boiled potatoes and beets. Some persons serve the pork, and the fat from it, in a gravy boat so it can be added as relished.

SAUCES

The art of preparing savory gravies and sauces is more important in connection with the serving of the cheaper meats than in connection with the cooking of the more expensive.

There are a few general principles underlying the making of all sauces or gravies whether the liquid used is water, milk, stock, tomato juice, or some combination of these. For ordinary gravy 2 level tablespoonfuls of flour or 1½ tablespoonfuls of cornstarch or arrow root is sufficient to thicken a cupful of liquid. This is true excepting when, as in the recipe on page 23 the flour is browned. In this case about one-half tablespoonful more should be allowed, for browned flour does not thicken so well as unbrowned. The fat used may be butter or the drippings from the meat, the allowance being 2 tablespoonfuls to a cup of liquid.

The easiest way to mix the ingredients is to heat the fat, add the flour, and cook until the mixture ceases to bubble, and then to add the liquid. This is a quick method and by using it there is little danger of getting lumpy gravy. Many persons, however, think it is not a wholesome method and prefer the old-fashioned one of thickening that gravy by means of flour mixed with a little cold water. The latter method is, of course, not practicable for brown gravies.

The good flavor of browned flour is often overlooked. If flour is cooked in fat until it is a dark brown color a distinctive and very agreeable flavor is obtained. This flavor combines very well with that of currant jelly, and a little jelly added to a brown gravy is a great improvement. The flavor of this should not be combined with that of onions or other highly flavored vegetables. A recipe for a dish which is made with brown sauce follows:

MOCK VENISON

Cut cold mutton into thin slices and heat in a brown sauce, made accordingly to the following proportions:

> 2 tablespoonfuls butter.
> 2 tablespoonfuls flour.
> 1 tablespoonful of bottled meat sauce (whichever is preferred).
> 1 tablespoonful red-currant jelly.
> 1 cupful water or stock.

Brown the flour in the butter, add the water or stock slowly, and keep stirring. Then add the jelly and meat sauce and let the mixture boil up well.

CHAPTER XV

HOUSEHOLD RECIPES

(Arranged Alphabetically)

"The woman's work for her own home is to secure its order, comfort, and loveliness."
JOHN RUSKIN—*Sesame and Lilies.*

The following recipes are tried and approved ones, useful for housecleaning, laundry work, etc. In a number of instances they give instruction in the making of commodities, such as soap, which are unusually purchased in the stores, but which, if made at home will cost less money, and be of better quality. They are arranged alphabetically for ease of reference:

ANTS—TO GET RID OF

Wash the shelves with salt and water; sprinkle salt in their paths. To keep them out of safes, set the legs of the safe on tin cups; keep the cups filled with water.

BARRELS—TO CLEAN

The ordinary way of washing a barrel is with boiling water, and when cool examining it with a light inside. If there be any sour or musty smell, however, lime must be used to remove it. Break the lime into lumps, and put it in the cask to dry (it will take from 3 to 4 lbs. for each cask), then pour in as many gallons of boiling water as there are pounds of lime, and bung. Roll the cask about now and then, and after a few hours wash it out, steam it, and let it cool.

BED-BUGS—TO KILL

For bed-bugs nothing is so good as the white of eggs and quicksilver. A thimbleful of quick-silver to the white of each egg; heat until well mixed; apply with a feather.

FEATHER-BEDS—TO CLEANSE
WITHOUT EMPTYING

On a hot, clear summer day, lay the bed upon a scaffold; wash it well with soap-suds upon both sides, rubbing it hard with a stiff brush; pour several gallons of hot water upon the bed slowly, and let it drip through. Rinse with clear water; remove it to a dry part of the scaffold to dry; beat, and turn it two or three times during the day. Sun until perfectly dry. The feathers may be emptied in barrels, washed in soap-suds, and rinsed; then spread in an unoccupied room and dried, or put in bags made of thin sleazy cloth, and kept in the sun until dry. The quality of feathers can be much improved by attention of this kind.

CLOTHES—TO BLEACH

Dissolve a handful of refined borax in ten gallons of water; boil the clothes in it. To whiten brown cloth, boil in weak lye, and expose day and night to the sun and night air; keep the clothes well sprinkled.

BOOKS—TO KEEP MICE FROM

Sprinkle a little Cayenne pepper in the cracks at the back of the shelves of the bookcase.

BOARDS—TO SCOUR

Mix in a saucer three parts of fine sand and one part of lime; dip the scrubbing-brush into this and use it instead of soap. This will remove grease and whiten the boards, while at the same time it will destroy all insects. The boards should be well rinsed with clean water. If they are very greasy, they should be well covered over in places with a coating of fuller's earth moistened with boiling water, which should be left on 24 hours before they are scoured as above directed. In washing boards never rub crosswise, but always with the grain.

BOOKS—TO PRESERVE FROM DAMP

A few drops of strong perfumed oil, sprinkled in the bookcase will preserve books from damp and mildew.

BOOKS—TO CLEAN

Books may be cleaned with a little dry bread crumbled up and rubbed gently, but firmly, over with the open hand. Cloth covers may be washed with a sponge dipped in a mixture made from the white of an egg beaten to a stiff froth and afterwards allowed to settle. To clean grease marks from books, dampen the marks with a little benzine, place a piece of blotting-paper on each side of the page, and pass a hot iron over the top.

BRASS—TO CLEAN

Dissolve 1 oz. of oxalic acid in one pint of soft water. Rub it on the brass with a piece of flannel, and polish with another dry piece. This solution should be kept in a bottle labeled "poison," and the bottle well shaken before it is used, which should be only occasionally, for in a general way the brass should be cleaned with pulverized rottenstone, mixed into a liquid state with oil of turpentine. Rub this on with a piece of soft leather, leave for a few minutes; then wipe it off with a soft cloth. Brass treated generally with the latter, and occasionally with the former mode of cleaning will look most beautiful. A very good general polish for brass may be made of ½ a lb. of rottenstone and 1 oz. of oxalic acid, with as much water as will make it into a stiff paste. Set this paste on a plate in a cool oven to dry, pound it very fine, and apply a little of the powder, moistened with sweet oil, to the brass with a piece of leather, polishing with another leather or an old silk handkerchief. This powder should also be labelled "poison."

BRITANNIA METAL—TO CLEAN

Articles made of what is usually called Britannia metal may be kept in order by the frequent use of the following composition: ½ a lb. of finely-powdered whiting, a wine-glass of sweet oil, a tablespoonful of soft soap, and ½ an oz. of yellow soap melted in water. Add to these in mixing sufficient spirits—gin or spirits of wine—to make the compound the consistency of cream. This cream should be applied with a sponge or soft flannel, wiped off with soft linen rags, and the article well polished with a leather; or they may be cleaned with only oil and soap in the following manner: Rub the articles with sweet oil on a piece of woolen cloth; then wash well with strong soap-and-water; rub them dry, and polish with a soft leather and whiting. The polish thus given will last for a long time.

BRUSHES—TO WASH

Dissolve a piece of soda in some hot water, allowing a piece the size of a walnut to a quart of water. Put the water into a basin, and, after combing out the hair from the brushes, dip them, bristles downward, into the water and out again, keeping the backs and handles as free from the water as possible. Repeat this until the bristles look clean; then rinse the brushes in a little cold water; shake them well, and wipe the handles and backs with a towel, but not the bristles, and set the brushes to dry in the sun, or near the fire; but take care not to put them too close to it. Wiping the bristles of a brush makes them soft, as does also the use of soap.

CARPETS—TO CLEAN

Shake the carpet well; tack it down, and wash it upon the floor; the floor should be very clean; use cold soap suds; to three gallons add half a tumbler of beef-gall; this will prevent the colors from fading. Should there be grease spots, apply a mixture of beef-gall, fuller's-earth, and water enough to form a paste; put this on before tacking the carpet down. Use tacks inserted in small leather caps. Carpets in bedrooms and stair-carpets may be kept clean by being brushed with a soft hairbrush frequently, and, as occasion requires, being taken up and shaken. Larger carpets should be swept carefully with a whisk-brush or hand-brush of hair, which is far better, especially in the case of fine-piled carpets. Thick carpets, as Axminster and Turkey, should always be brushed one way.

CARPETS—TO LAY

This can hardly be well done without the aid of a proper carpet-fork or stretcher. Work the carpet the length way of the material, which ought to be made up the length way of the room. Nail sides as you go along, until you are quite sure that the carpet is fully stretched, and that there is no fold anywhere in the length of it.

STAIR-CARPET—TO CLEAN

Make stair-carpet longer than necessary, and change it so that it will not cover the steps in the same way each time of putting down. Moved about in this way, the carpet will last much longer. Clean the rods with oxalic acid. They should be kept bright.

CHIMNEY ON FIRE

Close all doors and windows tightly, and hold a wet blanket in front of the fire to prevent any draught going up the chimney.

CHINA OR GLASS—TO WASH

Wash in plenty of hot soap suds; have two vessels, and in one rinse in hot water. Turn upon waiters, and let the articles drip before being wiped. Use linen towels for wiping.

CHINA AND GLASS—CEMENT FOR

Dissolve 1 oz. of gum-mastic in a quantity of highly-rectified spirits of wine; then soften 1 oz. of isinglass in warm water, and, finally, dissolve it in alcohol, till it forms a thick jelly. Mix the isinglass and gun-mastic together, adding ¼ of an oz. of finely-powdered gum ammoniac; put the whole into an earthen vessel and in a warm place, till they are thoroughly incorporated together; pour it into a small bottle, and cork it down for use.

In using it, dissolve a small piece of the cement in a silver teaspoon over a lighted candle. The broken pieces of glass or china being warmed, and touched with the now liquid cement, join the parts neatly together, and hold them in their places till the cement has set; then wipe away the cement adhering to the edge of the joint, and leave it for twelve hours without touching it; the joint will be as strong as the china itself, and if neatly done, it will show no joining. It is essential that neither of the pieces be wetted either with hot or cold water.

CLOTHES—CARE OF

Woolen dresses may be laid out on a table and brushed all over; but in general, even in woolen fabrics, the lightness of the tissues renders brushing unsuitable to dresses, and it is better to remove the dust from the folds by beating them lightly with a handkerchief or thin cloth. Silk dresses should never be brushed, but rubbed with a piece of merino or other soft material, of a similar color to the silk, kept for the purpose. Summer dresses of muslin, and other light materials, simply require shaking; but if the muslin be tumbled, it must be ironed afterwards.

If the feathers have suffered from damp, they should be held near the fire for a few minutes, and restored to their natural state by the hand or a soft brush, or re-curled with a blunt knife, dipped in very hot water. Furs and feathers not in constant use should be wrapped up in linen washed in lye. From May to September they are subject to being made the depository of moth-eggs.

CLOTHES—TO BRUSH

Fine clothes require to be brushed lightly, and with a rather soft brush, except where mud is to be removed, when a hard one is necessary; previously beat the clothes lightly to dislodge the dirt. Lay the garment on a table, and brush in the direction of the nap. Having brushed it properly, turn the sleeves back to the collar, so that the folds may come to the elbow-joints; next turn the lapels or sides back over the folded sleeves; then lay the skirts over level with the collar, so that the crease may fall about the center, and double only half over the other, so that the fold comes in the center of the back.

CLOTHES—TO REMOVE SPOTS
AND STAINS FROM

To remove grease spots from cotton or woolen materials, absorbent pastes, and even common soap, are used, applied to the spot when dry. When the colors are not fast, place a layer of fuller's-earth or pulverized potter's clay over the spot, and press with a very hot iron. For silks, moirés and plain or brocaded satins, pour two drops of rectified spirits of wine over the spot, cover with a linen cloth, and press with a hot iron, changing the linen instantly. The spot will look tarnished, for a portion of the grease still remains; this will be removed entirely by a little sulphuric ether, dropped on the spot, and a very little rubbing. If neatly done, no perceptible mark or circle will remain; nor will the lustre of the richest silk be changed, the union of the two liquids operating with no injurious effects from rubbing. *Eau-de-Cologne* will also remove grease from cloth and silk. Fruit spots are removed from white and fast-colored cottons by the use of chloride of soda. Commence by cold-soaping the article, then touch the spot with a hair-pencil or feather dipped in the chloride, and dip immediately into cold water, to prevent the texture if the article being injured. Fresh ink spots are removed by a few drops of hot water being poured on immediately after applying the chloride of soda. By the same process, iron-mould in linen or calico may be removed, dipping immediately in cold water to prevent injury to the fabric. Wax dropped on a shawl, table-cover, or cloth dress, is easily discharged by applying spirits of wine; syrups or preserved fruits, by washing in lukewarm water with a dry cloth, and pressing the spot between two folds of clean linen.

CRAPE—TO RENOVATE

Place a little water in a tea-kettle and let it boil until there is plenty of steam from the spout; then, holding the crape with both hands, pass it to and fro several times through the steam, and it will be clean and look nearly equal to new.

COMBS—TO CLEAN

If it can be avoided, never wash combs, as the water often makes the teeth split, and the tortoise-shell or horn of which they are made, rough. Small brushes, manufactured purposely for cleaning combs, may be purchased at a trifling cost; the comb should be well brushed, and afterwards wiped with a cloth or towel.

CUPBOARDS, DAMP—TO DRY

Leave a quantity of quicklime in the cupboard for a few days, and the moisture will be entirely absorbed.

EGGS—TO PACK

Put into a butter firkin a thick layer of coarse dry salt, then a layer of eggs, with the small end down, another layer of salt, then eggs, and so on until the firkin is full. Cover and keep in a dry place. These eggs will keep put up in this way almost any length of time.

COAL-FIRE—TO LIGHT

Clear out all ash from the grate and lay a few cinders or small pieces of coal at the bottom in open order; over this a few pieces of paper, and over that again eight or ten pieces of dry wood; over the wood, a course of moderate-sized pieces of coal, taking care to leave hollow spaces between for air at the center; and taking care to lay the whole well back in the grate, so that the smoke may go up the chimney, and not into the room. This done, fire the paper with a match from below, and, if properly laid, it will soon burn up; the stream of flame from the wood and paper soon communicating to the coal and cinders, provided there is plenty of air at the center.

Another method of lighting a fire is sometimes practiced with advantage, the fire lighting from the top and burning down, in place of being lighted and burning up from below. This is arranged by laying the coals at the bottom, mixed with a few good-sized cinders, and the wood at the top, with another layer of coals and some paper over it; the paper is lighted in the usual way, and soon burns down to a good fire, with some economy of fuel, it is said.

FEATHERS—TO CLEAN

Cover the feathers with a paste made of pipe-clay, and water, rubbing them one way only. When quite dry, shake off all the powder and curl with a knife.

FLANNEL—TO WASH

Never rub soap upon it; make suds by dissolving the soap in warm water; rinse in warm water. Very cold or hot water will shrink flannel. Shake them out several minutes before hanging to dry. Blankets are washed in the same way.

FLEAS—TO DRIVE AWAY

Use pennyroyal tea or walnut leaves. Scatter them profusely in all infested places.

FLIES—TO DESTROY

A mixture of cream, sugar, and ground black pepper, in equal quantities, placed in saucers in a room infested with flies will destroy them. If a small quantity, say the equivalent of a teaspoonful of carbolic acid be poured on a hot shovel, it will drive the flies from the room. But screens should be used to prevent their entrance.

STEEL-FORKS—TO CLEAN

Have a small box filled with clean sand; mix with it a third the quantity of soft soap; clean the forks by sticking in the sand and withdrawing them rapidly, repeating the process until they are bright.

CUT-FLOWERS—TO PRESERVE

A bouquet of freshly-cut flowers may be preserved alive for a long time by placing them in a glass or vase with fresh water, in which a little charcoal has been steeped, or a small piece of camphor dissolved. The vase should be set upon a plate or dish, and covered with a bell glass, around the edges of which, when it comes in contact with the plate, a little water should be poured to exclude the air. To revive cut flowers, plunge the stems into boiling water, and by the time the water is cold, the flowers will have revived. Then cut the ends of the stems afresh, and place in fresh cold water.

FRUIT STAINS—TO REMOVE

Pour hot water on the spots; wet with ammonia or oxalic acid—a teaspoonful to a teacup of water.

FRUIT-TREES—TO PREVENT DEPREDATIONS OF

To preserve apple and other fruit trees from the depredations of rabbits, etc., and the ravages of insects, apply soft soap to the trunk and branches in March and September.

FURNITURE GLOSS—GERMAN

Cut ¼ of a lb. of yellow wax into small pieces and melt it in an earthen vessel, with 1 oz. of black rosin, pounded very fine. Stir in gradually, while these two ingredients are quite warm, 2 ozs. of oil of turpentine. Keep this composition well covered for use in a tin or earthen pot. A little of this gloss should be spread on a piece of coarse woolen cloth, and the furniture well rubbed with it; afterward it should be polished with a fine cloth.

FURNITURE POLISH

One pint of linseed oil, one wineglass of alcohol. Mix well together. Apply to the furniture with a fine rag. Rub dry with a soft cotton cloth, and polish with a silk cloth. Furniture is improved by washing it occasionally with soapsuds. Wipe dry, and rub over with very little linseed oil upon a clean sponge or flannel. Wipe polished furniture with silk. Separate dusting-cloths and brushes should be kept for highly polished furniture. When sweeping carpets and dusting walls always cover the furniture until the particles of dust floating in the air settle, then remove the covers and wipe with a silk or soft cotton cloth.

FURNITURE STAINS—TO REMOVE

Rub stains on furniture with cold-drawn linseed oil, then rub with alcohol. Remove ink stains with oxalic acid and water; wash off with milk. A hot iron held over stains upon furniture will sometimes remove them.

FURS—TO CLEAN

Moisten some bran with hot water; rub the fur with it, and dry with a flannel. Then rub with a piece of muslin and some dry bran.

GAS—TO DETECT A LEAK

Never take a light into the room or look for the leak with a light. Soap and water mixed, and applied with a brush to the pipe will commence to bubble if there is a leak. Send for the plumber at once.

GLASS—TO WASH

Great care is required in washing glasses. Two perfectly clean bowls are necessary—one for moderately hot and another for cold water. Wash the glasses well in the first, rinse them in the second, and turn them down on a linen cloth folded two or three times, to drain for a few minutes. When sufficiently drained, wipe with a cloth and polish with a finer one, doing so tenderly and carefully.

Decanters and water-jugs require very tender

treatment in cleaning. Fill about two-thirds with hot but not boiling water, and put in a few pieces of well-soaked brown paper; leave them thus for two or three hours; then shake the water up and down in the decanters; empty this out, rinse them well with clean, cold water, and put them in a rack to drain. When dry, polish them outside and inside, as far as possible, with a fine cloth. Fine shot or pieces of charcoal placed in a decanter with warm water and shaken for some time, will also remove stains. When this is not effective, fill the bottle with finely chopped potato skins. Cork tight, and let the bottle stand for three days. Empty and rinse thoroughly.

GLASS STOPPER—TO REMOVE

Wrap a hot cloth around the neck of the bottle, thus expanding it, or, if this is not effective, pour a little salad oil round the stopper, and place the bottle near the fire, then tap the stopper with a wooden instrument. The beat will cause the oil to work round the stopper, and it should be removed.

GREASE—TO REMOVE FROM A STONE HEARTH

Lay plenty of hot ashes; wash off (after the grease is out) with strong soap suds.

HARNESS BLACKING—FOR PRESERVING
THE LEATHER

Melt four ounces of mutton suet with twelve ounces of beeswax; add twelve ounces of sugar-candy, four ounces of soft soap dissolved in water, and two ounces of indigo, finely powdered. When melted and well mixed, add one-half pint of turpentine. Lay the lacking on the harness with a sponge, and polish off with a brush.

FELT-HATS—TO RENOVATE

Mix equal quantities of benzine and water, and after well brushing the hat, apply the mixture with a sponge.

HERBS—TO DRY

The right way in drying herbs for your kitchen and possible medicinal use is to gather them as soon as they begin to open their flowers, and to lay them on some netting in a dry shed or room where the air will get at them on all sides. Be sure they are dry and not moist when you cut or pick them, and free them from dirt and decayed leaves. After they are entirely dried out, put them in paper bags upon which you have written the name of the herb and the date of tying it up. Hang them where the air is dry and there is no chance of their moulding.

SAVORY HERBS—TO POWDER

Strip the leaves from the stalks, pound, sift out the coarse pieces, put the powder in bottles and cork tight. Label with exactness every bottle. If, for the convenience of instant use in gravies, soups, etc., you wish different herbs mixed, pound the leaves together when you make them into powders. Celery seed, dried lemon-peel, and other spicy things can thus be combined and ready for the moment's call.

ICE VAULT—TO MAKE

Dig a pit eight or ten feet square, and as deep in the cellar. Lay a double wall with brick; fill between with pulverized charcoal; cover the bottom also double with the same or tan-bark. If the pit is filled with ice, or nearly so, cover six inches with tan-bark; but if only a small quantity is in it, wrap well in a blanket, and over the opening in the pit lay a double bag of charcoal.

INK—TO REMOVE FROM LINEN

Scald in hot tallow. Let it cool; then wash in warm suds. Sometimes these stains can be removed by wetting the place in very sour buttermilk or lemon juice; rub salt over, and bleach in the sun.

INSECTS—TO KEEP AWAY

The common elder is a great safeguard against the devastations of insects. Scatter it around cucumber and squash-vines. Place it on the branches of plum and other fruit-trees subject to the ravages of insects.

IRONS—TO REMOVE RUST FROM

Scour with dry salt and beeswax.

JAPANNED WARE—TO CLEAN

Japanned tea-trays should not be washed in hot water if greasy, a little flour rubbed on with a bit of soft linen will give them a new look; if there are scratches, rub over a little olive oil.

JEWELRY—TO CLEAN

Jewels are generally wrapped up in cotton wool and kept in their cases; but they tarnish from exposure to the air and require cleaning. This is done by preparing clean soap-suds from fine toilet-soap. Dip any article of gold, silver, gilt or precious stones into this lye, and dry by brushing with a brush of soft hair, or a fine sponge; afterwards polish with a piece of fine cloth, and lastly, with a soft leather.

Gold or silver ornaments, and in general all articles of jewelry, may be dressed by dipping them in spirits of wine warmed in a shallow kettle, placed over a slow fire or hot plate. Silver ornaments should be kept in fine arrowroot, and completely covered with it.

KNIVES—TO CLEAN

Cover a small heavy table on block by tacking over it very tight soft leather or buckskin; pour over half he leather melted suet. Spread over this very fine pulverized bath brick; rub the knives (making rapid strokes) over this. Polish on the other side. Keep steel wrapped in buckskin. Knives should be cleaned every day they are used, and kept sharp. The handles of knives should never be immersed in water, as, after a time if treated in this way, the blades will loosen and the handles discolor. The blades should be put in a jug or vessel kept for the purpose, filled with hot soda water. This should be done as soon after the knives are used as possible, as stain and rust quickly sink into steel.

KNIVES—TO KEEP

Knives not in use will soon spoil. They are best kept in a box in which sifted quicklime has been placed, deep enough to admit of the blades being completely plunged into it. The lime must not touch the handles, which should be occasionally exposed to the air, to keep them from turning yellow.

BLACK LACE—TO REVIVE

Make some black tea, about the strength usual for drinking, and strain it off the leaves. Pour enough tea into a basin to cover the material, then squeeze the lace several times, but do not rub it. Dip it frequently into the tea, which will at length assume a dirty appearance. Have ready some weak gum-water and press the lace gently through it; then clap it for a quarter of an hour; after which, pin it to a towel in any shape which you wish it to take. When nearly dry, cover it with another towel and iron it with a cool iron. The lace, if previously sound and discolored only, will, after this process, look as good as new.

LAMPS—TO TRIM

In trimming lamps, let the wick be cut evenly all round; as, if left higher in one place than it is in another, it will cause it to smoke and burn badly. The lamp should then be filled with oil from a feeder and afterward well wiped with a cloth or rag. Small sticks, covered with wash-leather pads, are the best things to use for cleaning the inside of the chimney and a clean duster for polishing the outside. Chimneys should not be washed. The globe of a lamp should be occasionally washed in warm soap-and-water, then well rinsed in cold water, and either wiped dry or left to drain.

LEATHER—TO CLEAN

For fawn or yellow-colored leather, take a quart of skimmed milk, pour into it one ounce of sulphuric acid, and, when cold, add four ounces of hydrochloric acid, shaking the bottle gently until it ceases to emit white vapors; separate the coagulated from the liquid part, by straining through a sieve, and store it away till required. Clean the leather with a weak solution of oxalic acid, washing it off immediately, and when dry apply the composition with a sponge.

TABLE LINEN—CARE OF

Table-cloths, towels and napkins should be kept faultlessly white; table-cloths and napkins starched; if the latter are fringed, whip the fringe until straight. After using a table-cloth, lay it in the same folds; put it in a close place where dust will not reach it, and lay a heavy weight upon it.

Napkins may be used the second time, if they are so marked that each person gets the napkin previously used.

LINEN—TO GLAZE

The gloss, or enamel, as it is sometimes called, is produced mainly by friction with a warm iron, and may be put on linen by almost any person. The linen to be glazed receives as much strong starch as it is possible to charge it with, then it is dried. To each pound of starch a piece of sperm or white wax, about the size of a walnut, is usually added. When ready to be ironed, the linen is laid upon the table and moistened very lightly on the surfaces with a clean wet cloth. It is then ironed in the usual way with a flatiron, and is ready for the glossing operation. For this purpose a peculiar heavy flatiron, rounded at the bottom, as bright as a mirror, is used. It is pressed firmly upon the linen and rubbed with much force, and this frictional action puts on the gloss. "Elbow grease" is the principal secret connected with the art of glossing linen.

MACKINTOSH—TO REPAIR

Shred finely some pure India-rubber, and dissolve it in naphtha to the consistency of a stiff paste. Apply the cement to each side of the part to be joined, and leave a cold iron upon it until dry.

LINEN—TO REMOVE IRON
MOULD FROM

Oxalic acid and hot water will remove iron-mould; so also will common sorrel, bruised in a mortar and rubbed on the spots. In both cases the linen should be well washed after the remedy has been applied, either in clear water or a strong solution of cream of tartar and water. Repeat if necessary, and dry in the sun.

MAHOGANY—TO TAKE OUT
MARKS FROM

The whitest stain, left on a mahogany table by a jug of boiling water, or a very hot dish, may be removed by rubbing in oil, and afterward pouring a little spirits of wine on the spot and rubbing with a soft cloth.

MARBLE—TO CLEAN

Wash with soda, water, and beef-gall. Or mix together one part blue-stone, three parts whiting, one part soda, and three parts soft soap; boil together ten minutes; stir constantly. Spread this over the marble; let it lie half and hour; wash it off with soap-suds; wipe dry with flannel. Repeat if necessary. Stains that cannot be removed in any other way may be tried with oxalic acid water; but this should be used carefully, and not allowed to remain long at a time.

MATTING—TO WASH

Use salt in the water, and wipe dry.

MILDEW—TO REMOVE

When the clothes are washed and ready to boil, pin jimson weed leaves upon the place. Put a handful of the leaves on the bottom of the kettle; lay the stained part next to them. Green tomatoes and salt, sour buttermilk, lemon juice, soap and chalk, are all good; expose to the sun.

Another way: Two ounces of chloride of lime; pour on it a quarter of boiling water; add three quarts of cold water. Steep the cloth in it twelve hours.

MIRRORS—TO CLEAN

Remove, with a damp sponge, fly stains and other soils (the sponge may be damped with water or spirits of wine). After this dust the surface with the finest sifted whiting or powder-blue, and polish it with a silk handkerchief or soft cloth. Snuff of candle, if quite free from grease, is an excellent polish for the looking-glass.

MOTHS—TO PREVENT THEM GETTING INTO CARPETS, ETC.

Strew camphor under a carpet; pack with woolen goods. If moths are in a carpet, lay over it a cotton or linen cloth, and iron with a hot iron. Oil all cracks in storerooms, closets, safes, with turpentine, or a mixture of alcohol and corrosive sublimate; this drives off vermin.

Place pieces of camphor, cedar-wood, Russia leather, tobacco-leaves, boy-myrtle, or anything else strongly aromatic in the drawers or boxes where furs or other things to be preserved from moths are kept, and they will never take harm.

OIL-CLOTH OR LINOLEUM—TO WASH

Take equal parts of skimmed milk and water; wipe dry; never use soap. Varnish oil-cloths once a year. After being varnished, they should be perfectly dry before being used.

PAINT—TO CLEAN

Dirty paint should never be wiped with a cloth; but the dust should be loosened with a pair of bellows, and then removed with a dusting-brush. If very dirty, wash the paint lightly with a sponge or soft flannel dipped in weak soda-and-water, or in pearl-ash and water. The sponge or flannel must be used nearly dry, and the portion of paint gone over must immediately be rinsed with a flannel and clean water; both soda and pearl-ash, if suffered to remain on, will injure the paint. The operation of washing should, therefore, be done as quickly as possible, and two persons should be employed; one to follow and dry the paint with soft rags, as soon as the other has scoured off the dirt and washed away the soda. No scrubbing-brush should ever be used on paint.

PAINT—TO DISPERSE
THE SMELL OF

Place some sulphuric acid in a basin of water and let it stand in the room where the paint is. Change the water daily.

PAINT—TO REMOVE
FROM CLOTHING

Rub immediately with a rough rag wetted with turpentine.

OIL PAINTINGS—TO CLEAN

Rub a freshly cut slice of potato damped in cold water over the picture. Wipe off the lather with a soft, damp sponge, and then finish with luke-warm water, and dry, and polish with a piece of soft silk that has been washed.

PAPER HANGING—TO MAKE
PASTE FOR

Mix flour and water to the consistency of cream, and boil. A few cloves added in the boiling will prevent the paste going sour.

PEARS—TO KEEP FOR
WINTER USE

Lay the pears on a shelf in a dry, cool place. Set them stems up and so far apart that they do not touch one another. Allow the air to move freely in the room in which they lie. Layers of paper or of straw make a soft bed, but the less the pear touches the shelf or resting-place the better for its keeping.

PICTURE FRAMES—TO KEEP
FLIES FROM

Brush them over with water in which onions have been boiled.

GILT PICTURE FRAMES—
TO BRIGHTEN

Take sufficient sulphur to give a golden tinge to about one and one-half pints of water, and in this boil four or five bruised onions. Strain off the liquid when cold, and with it wash with a soft brush any gilding which requires restoring, and when dry it will come out as bright as new work. Frames may also be brightened in the following manner: Beat up the white of eggs with soda, in the proportion of three ounces of eggs to one ounce of soda. Blow off as much dust as possible from the frames, and paint them over with a soft brush dipped in the mixture. They will immediately come out fresh and bright.

RATS—TO DESTROY

Set traps and put a few drops of rhodium inside; they are fond of it. Cats are, however, the most reliable rat-traps. There is no difficulty in poisoning rats, but they often die in the walls, and create a dreadful odor, hard to get rid of. When poisoning is attempted, remove or cover all water vessels, even the well or cistern.

RIBBONS—TO WASH

If there are grease spots, rub the yolk of an egg upon them, on the wrong side; let it dry. Lay it upon a clean cloth, and wash upon each side with a sponge; press on the wrong side. If very much soiled, wash in bran-water; add to the water in which it is rinsed a little muriate of tin to set red, oil of vitrol for green, blue, maroon, and bright yellow.

RUST—TO PRESERVE FROM

Make a strong paste of fresh lime and water, and with a fine brush smear it as thickly as possible over all the polished surface requiring preservation. By this simple means, all the grates and fire-irons in an empty house may be kept for months free from harm, without further care or attention.

RUST—TO REMOVE FROM
POLISHED STEEL

Rub the spots with soft animal fat; lay the articles by; wrap in thick paper two days; clean off the grease with flannel; rub the spots well with fine rotten-stone and sweet oil; polish with powdered emery and soft leather, or with magnesia or fine chalk.

RUST—TO REMOVE FROM IRON UTENSILS

Rub sweet oil upon them. Let it remain two days; cover with finely-powdered lime; rub this off with leather in a few hours. Repeat if necessary.

To prevent their rusting when not in use: Mix half a pound of lime with a quart of warm water; add sweet oil until it looks like cream. Rub the article with this; when dry, wrap in paper or put over another coat. See also IRONS.

RUST AND INK STAINS—TO REMOVE

Put half an ounce of oxalic acid in a pint of water. Dip the stain in the water, and apply the acid as often as necessary. Wash very soon, in half an hour at least, or the cloth will be injured by the acid. Preserve in bottle marked "Poison." This also cleans brass beautifully.

RUSTED SCREWS—TO LOOSEN

Boil scorched articles in milk and turpentine, half a pound of soap, half a gallon of milk. Lay in the sun.

RUSTED SCREWS—TO LOOSEN

Pour a small quantity of paraffin round the top of the screw. When sufficient time has been allowed for the oil to sink in, the screw can be easily removed.

SEALING-WAX FOR BOTTLES, JARS, ETC.

Three-fourths rosin, one-fourth beeswax; melt. Or use half a pound of rosin, the same quantity of red sealing-wax, and a half an ounce of beeswax; melt, and as it froths up, stir it with a tallow candle. Use new corks; trim (after driving them in securely) even with the bottle, and dip the necks in this cement.

SHIRTS—TO IRON

Use for ironing shirts a bosom-board, made of seasoned wood a foot wide, one and a half long, and an inch thick; cover it well by tacking over very tight two or three folds of flannel, according to the thickness of the flannel. Cover it lastly with Canton flannel; this must be drawn over very tight, and tacked well to prevent folds when in use. Make slips of fine white cotton cloth; put a clean one on every week. A skirt-board must be made in the same way for ironing dresses; five feet long, tapering from two feet at one end to a foot and a half at the other, the large end should be round. A clean slip should be upon it whenever used. A similar but smaller board should be kept for ironing gentlemen's summer pants. Keep fluting and crimping irons, a small iron for ruffles, and a polishing-iron.

RUSSET SHOES—TO POLISH

Remove stains with lemon juice, and polish with beeswax dissolved in turpentine.

SHOES—TO PREVENT
FROM CRACKING

Saturate a piece of flannel in boiled linseed oil and rub it well over the soles and round the edges of the shoes, then stand them, soles upward, to dry.

SILK—TO RENOVATE

Sponge faded silks with warm water and soap; then rub them with a dry cloth on a flat board; afterward iron them on the inside with a smoothing-iron. Old black silks may be improved by sponging with spirits. In this case, the ironing may be done on the right side, thin paper being spread over to prevent glazing.

SILK AND SATIN—TO CLEAN

Pin the breadths on a soft blanket; then take some stale breadcrumbs, and mix with them a little powder-blue. Rub this thoroughly and carefully over the whole surface with the hand or piece of clean linen; shake it off and wipe with soft cloths. Satin may be brushed the way of the nap with a clean, soft, hair-brush.

SILK—TO TAKE STAINS FROM

Mix two ounces of essence of lemon and one ounce of turpentine. Grease and other spots in silks are to be rubbed gently with a linen rag dipped in this mixture.

SILKS—TO WASH

For a dress to be washed, the seams of a skirt do not require to be ripped apart, though it must be removed from the band at the waist, and the lining taken from the bottom. Trimmings or drapings, where there are deep folds, the bottom of which is very difficult to reach, should be undone, so as to remain flat. A black silk dress, without being previously washed, may be refreshed by being soaked during twenty-four hours in soft, clear water, clearness in the water being indispensable. If dirty the black dress may be previously washed. When very old and rusty, a pint of alcohol should be mixed with each gallon of water. This addition is an improvement under any circumstances, whether the silk be previously washed or not. After soaking, the dress should be hung up to drain dry without being wrung. The mode of washing silks is this: The article should be laid upon a clean, smooth table. A flannel just wetted with lukewarm water should be well soaped, and the surface of the silk rubbed one way with it, care being taken that this rubbing is quite even. When the dirt has disappeared, the soap must be washed off with a sponge and plenty of cold water, of which the sponge must be made to imbibe as much as possible. As soon as one side is finished, the other must be washed precisely in the same manner. Let it be understood that not more of either surface must be done at a time than can be spread perfectly flat upon the table, and the hand can conveniently reach; likewise the soap must be quite sponged off one portion before the soaped flannel is applied to another portion. Silks, when washed, should always be dried in the shade, on a linen horse, and alone. If black or dark blue, they will be improved if they are placed on a table when dry, and well sponged with alcohol.

SILVER—TO POLISH

Boil soft rags for five minutes (nothing is better for the purpose than the tops of old cotton stockings) in a mixture of new milk and ammonia. As soon as they are taken out, wring them for a moment in cold water, and dry before the fire. With these rags rub the silver briskly as soon as it has been well washed and dried after daily use. A most beautiful deep polish will be produced, and the silver will require nothing more than merely to be dusted with a leather or a dry, soft cloth before it is again put on the table.

SILVER—TO CLEAN

Wash in hot soap suds (use the silver soap if convenient); then clean with a paste of whiting and water, or whiting and alcohol. Polish with buckskin. If silver was always washed in hot suds, rinsed well, and wiped dry, it would seldom need anything else.

SILVER—TO REMOVE STAINS FROM

Steep the silver in lye four hours; then cover thick with whiting wet with vinegar; let this dry; rub with dry whiting; and polish with dry wheat bran.

Egg-stains may be removed from silver by rubbing with table salt.

SOAK CLOTHES
FOR WASHING—TO

Take a gallon of water, one pound of sal soda, and one pound of soap; boil one hour, then add on tablespoonful of spirits of turpentine. Put the clothes to soak over night; next morning soap them well with the mixture. Boil well one hour; rinse in three waters; add a little bluing to the last water.

SOFT SOAP—TO MAKE

The ashes should be of hardwood (hickory is best), and kept dry. When put in the hopper, mix a bushel of unslacked lime with ten bushels of ashes; put in a layer of ashes; then one slight sprinkling of lime; wet each layer with water (rain water is best). A layer of straw should be put upon the bottom of the hopper before the ashes are put in. An opening in the side or bottom for the lye to drip through, and a trough or vessel under to receive the lye. When the lye is strong enough to bear up an egg, so as to show the size of a dime above the surface, it is ready for making soap; until it is, pour it back into the hopper, and let it drip through again. Add water to the ashes in such quantities as may be needed. Have the vessel very clean in which the soap is to be made. Rub the pot over with corn meal after washing it, and if it is at all discolored, rub it over with more until the vessel is perfectly clean. Melt three pounds of clean grease; add to it a gallon of weak lye, a piece of alum the size of a walnut. Let this stew until well mixed. If strong lye is put to the grease, at first it will not mix well with the grease. In an hour add three gallons of strong hot lye; boil briskly, and stir frequently; stir one way. After it has boiled several hours, cool a spoonful upon a plate; if it does not jelly, add a little water; if this causes it to jelly, then add water to the kettle. Stir quickly while the water is poured in until it ropes on the stick. As to the quantity of water required to make it jelly, judgment must be used; the quantity will depend upon circumstances. It will be well to take some in a bowl, and notice what proportion of water is used to produce this effect.

To harden it: Add a quart of salt to this quantity of soap; let it boil quick ten minutes; let it cool. Next day cut it out. This is now ready for washing purposes.

BROWN TAR SOAP—TO MAKE

Take eight gallons of soft soap, two quarts of salt, and one pound of rosin, pulverized; mix, and boil half an hour. Turn it in a tub to cool.

SOAP-POTASH—TO MAKE

Six pounds of potash, five pounds of grease, and a quarter of a pound of powdered rosin; mix all well in a pot, and, when warm, pour on ten pounds of boiling water. Boil until thick enough.

SOAP FOR CLEANING SILVER, ETC.— TO MAKE

One bar of turpentine soap, three table-spoonfuls of spirits of turpentine, half a tumbler of water. Let it boil ten minutes. Add six tablespoonfuls of ammonia. Make a suds of this, and wash silver with it.

SPERMACETI—TO REMOVE

Scrape it off; put brown paper on the spot and press with hot iron.

ACID STAINS—TO REMOVE

Apply ammonia to neutralize the acid; after which apply chloroform. This will remove paints from garments when benzine has failed.

STARCH—TO PREPARE

Wet two tablespoonfuls of starch to a smooth paste with cold water; pour to it a pint of boiling water; put it on the fire; let it boil, stirring frequently until it looks transparent; this will probably require half an hour. Add a piece of spermaceti as large as half a nutmeg, or as much salt, or loaf sugar—this will prevent the starch from sticking to the iron.

STARCH—COLD-WATER

Mix the starch to a smooth cream with cold water, then add borax dissolved in boiling water in the proportion of a dessertspoonful to a teacupful of starch.

MUSLINS—TO STARCH

Add to the starch for fine muslins a little white gum Arabic. Keep a bottle of it ready for use. Dissolve two ounces in a pint of hot water; bottle it; use as may be required, adding it to the starch. Muslins, calicoes, etc., should never be stiffer than when new. Rice-water and isinglass stiffen very thin muslins better than starch.

TAR AND PITCH—TO REMOVE

Grease the place with lard or sweet oil. Let it remain a day and night; then wash in suds. If silk or worsted, rub the stain with alcohol.

Paraffin will remove tar from the hands.

UMBRELLAS—CARE OF

An umbrella should not be folded up when it is wet. Let it stand with handle downwards, so that the wet can run off the ends of the ribs, instead of running towards the ferrule and rusting that part of the umbrella.

VELVET—TO RENEW

Hold the velvet, pile downwards, over the boiling water, in which ammonia is dissolved, double the velvet (pile inwards) and fold it lightly together.

WALL-PAPER—TO CLEAN

Tie cotton upon a long stick; brush the walls well with this. When soiled, turn it, or rub the walls with stale loaf bread. Split the loaf, and turn the soft spot to the wall.

WHITEWASH—TO MAKE

Put half a bushel of unslacked lime in a barrel;

cover it with hot water; stir occasionally, and keep the vessel well covered. When slacked, strain into another barrel through a sieve. Put a pound of glue in a glue-pot; melt it over a slow fire until dissolved. Soak the glue in cold water before putting the pot over the fire. Dissolve a peck of salt in boiling water. Make a thin paste of three pounds of ground rice boiled half an hour. Stir to this half a pound of Spanish whiting. Now add the rice paste to the lime; stir it in well; then the glue; mix well; cover the barrel, and let it stand twenty-four hours. When ready to use, it should be put on hot. It makes a durable wash for outside walls, planks, etc., and may be colored. Spanish brown will make it red or pink, according to the quantity used. A delicate tinge of this is very pretty for inside walls. Lampblack in small quantities will make slate color. Finely pulverized clay mixed with Spanish brown, makes lilac. Yellow chrome or yellow ochre makes yellow. Green must not be used; lime destroys the color, and makes the whitewash peel.

WINDOWS—TO WASH

Wash well with soap suds; rinse with warm water; rub dry with linen, and finish by polishing with soft dry paper. A fine polish is given to window-glass by brushing it over with a paste of whiting. Let it dry, rub off with paper or cloth, and with a clean, dry brush, remove every particle of the whiting from the corners. Once a year will be altogether sufficient for this.

THE END